HEAR DAT
NEW ORLEANS

HEAR DAT

NEW ORLEANS

*A Guide to the Rich Musical Heritage
and Lively Current Scene*

MICHAEL MURPHY

PHOTOGRAPHS BY MARC PAGANI

THE COUNTRYMAN PRESS
A DIVISION OF W. W. NORTON & COMPANY
INDEPENDENT PUBLISHERS SINCE 1923

Printed in the United States of America

For information about permission to reproduce selections from this book, write to Permissions, The Countryman Press, 500 Fifth Avenue, New York, NY 10110

For information about special discounts for bulk purchases, please contact W. W. Norton Special Sales at specialsales@wwnorton.com or 800-233-4830

The Countryman Press
www.countrymanpress.com

A division of W. W. Norton & Company, Inc.
500 Fifth Avenue, New York, NY 10110
www.wwnorton.com

Library of Congress Cataloging-in-Publication Data

Names: Murphy, Michael, 1954- author.
Title: Hear dat New Orleans : a guide to the rich musical heritage & lively
   current scene / Michael Murphy.
Description: Woodstock, VT : The Countryman Press, 2016. | Includes
   bibliographical references and index.
Identifiers: LCCN 2016001249 | ISBN 9781581573169 (pbk. : alk. paper)
Subjects: LCSH: Popular music—Louisiana—New Orleans—History and criticism.
   | New Orleans (La.)—Guidebooks.
Classification: LCC ML3477.8.N44 M87 2016 | DDC 780.9763/35—dc23 LC record
available at http://lccn.loc.gov/2016001249

10 9 8 7 6 5 4 3 2 1

My music is homegrown from the garden of New Orleans. Music is everything to me short of breathing. Music has a role to lift you up—not to be escapist but to take you out of misery.

—Allen Toussaint

DEDICATION

Mere weeks after submitting the manuscript for *Hear Dat*, Allen Toussaint passed away after a concert in Madrid. He had earlier been gracious, as he was always gracious to everyone he met, to respond to my request to contribute to the Overture / Introduction of this book. I contacted my editor immediately that we had to make 11th-hour changes to the book or we'd come off ridiculously uninformed or worse, horrendously calloused.

In death, Allen Toussaint felt irreplaceable. New Orleans carried a certain gloom that we had all lost something essential. We had. But one of the driving principles of Mr. Toussaint's life was to build upon and carry on to a new generation the great tradition of New Orleans musicians like Professor Longhair and James Booker and that distinctively New Orleans weird rumba-boogie beat.

No one will ever be able to pull off styling socks and sandals the way Mr. Toussaint could, just as we won't see another Uncle Lionel strolling the streets resplendent in his many hats, walking canes, and watch draped across his hand, nor will there ever be a smile as bright as Louis Armstrong's. But their music lives on. Their music will touch, comfort, or energize listeners not yet born.

Dedicating this book is easy. To the musicians past, present, and future who inspire and are inspired by our music and who give New Orleans its essential and utterly unique soul.

"Through pestilence, hurricanes, and conflagrations the people continued to sing. They sang through the long oppressive years of conquering the swampland and fortifying the town against the ever threatening Mississippi. They are singing today. An irrepressible joie de vivre maintains the unbroken thread of music through the air."

—Lura Robinson

CONTENTS

Phtotographs in the Carol M. Highsmith Archive, Library of Congress, Prints and Photographs Division

INTRODUCTION

New Orleans is the heart, soul, and music of America.

—Lenny Kravitz

Several tales prevail as to where and how *one* of New Orleans's nicknames, the Big Easy, originated. Some assume it derives from the slow and easy way New Orleanians choose to live their lives. A New Orleans astrologer, Lynn Wilson, said of the city, "New Orleans's value to the world lies in its charming dysfunctionality. The world doesn't need more Atlantas."

However, the most consistent and reliable derivation seems to come from "back in the day," when musicians used to ride the rails looking for paying gigs in New York, Chicago, Memphis, and elsewhere. Musicians shared the sentiment that New Orleans was the #1 place to go. They tabbed the city the Big Easy because there were so many bars, clubs, dance halls, and juke joints that any halfway decent musician would always have an easy time finding work.

The same is true today. The first thing visitors often ask is, "Where can I go to hear live music?" A better question would be, "Where can I go and not hear music?" Music is everywhere in this city. It practically bubbles up from the streets, as famously claimed by Ellis Marsalis, jazz pianist and patriarch of the musical royal family in New Orleans.

From the time you wake up to a jazz brunch (and hear street musicians on the way there) until the last club closes along Frenchmen Street past three in the morning, live music will be as much a part of your day as eating, drinking, and buying things you don't need.

Music will accompany your meal at restaurants like Palm Court Jazz Café, Little Gem Saloon, The Bombay Club, and Bacchanal, among many others. It will be played in your hotel lobby if you stay at The Columns Hotel, Hotel Monteleone, Irvin Mayfield's Jazz Playhouse inside the Royal Sonesta, and the Davenport Lounge inside the Ritz-Carlton. At least four, sometimes five nights a week, you can go bowling while listening to some of the city's best musicians at the Rock 'n' Bowl. The Grammy-nominated Dukes of Dixieland play nightly for the dinner cruise aboard the Steamboat Natchez.

Bars, juke joints, and clubs with live music number well over a hundred venues in New Orleans. Some spots, such as Tipitina's and Preservation Hall, are as famous as any musician who plays there. The amazing part is that even with the immense variety of options each night, and the weekly or thrice weekly appearance of any specific performer, the events are always sold out or standing room only. The Rebirth Brass Band fills Maple Leaf Bar every Tuesday night, as does The Hot 8 Brass Band every Sunday night at Howlin' Wolf. On Mondays, Charmaine Neville gives two performances at 8:00 p.m. and again at 10:00 inside Snug Harbor. Unless she's touring, Best Female Singer each of the last four years, Meschiya Lake, can be seen and heard several times each week as she performs regularly at The Spotted Cat, Chickie Wah Wah, Little Gem Saloon, and The Bombay Club.

Most spots will have a modest cover charge, usually 5 to 10 dollars. But there's also plenty of extremely good free music available. Wednesday at the Square is a 12-week series in Lafayette Square showcasing both local and national performers. Once, prior to living here, I happened upon Buddy Guy playing as part of the Lafayette Square series—for free. There is, additionally, a nine-week series of free concerts called Jazz in the Park held on Congo Square in Louis Armstrong Park. And for a $2 fee you can take a 15-minute ferry ride across the Mississippi River and join the free music series, Wednesdays on the Point, June through August near the Algiers Ferry Landing.

Street musicians line Royal Street and Jackson Square, playing for loose change and wrinkled bills. They are a cut above the buskers you'll find in any other city. Some current street bands like the Messy Cookers, the Slick Skillet Serenaders, and Tanya & Dorise have regular followers camp out in "their" section of the street. Before Meschiya Lake became four-time Best Female Vocalist and before Professor Longhair became the legendary heart and soul of New Orleans music, you could have heard them out playing for tips on the streets of the French Quarter.

Whenever you visit New Orleans, there will probably be a music festival going on, or at least a food festival or street fair that includes a heaping dose of live music. The Jazz & Heritage Festival, the French Quarter Festival, the Voodoo Music + Arts Experience, Crescent City Blues & BBQ Festival, Mid-City Bayou Boogaloo, and the Essence Festival are signature events each year. They draw as many as half a million visitors (per event) to New Orleans.

Entire books have been written just about Professor Longhair, Huey "Piano" Smith, and Ernie K-Doe (though K-Doe would have vigorously objected to the word *just* being used in the same sentence with his name). Jay Mazza has written a well-regarded book, *Not Just Another Thursday Night*, about one musician, Kermit Ruffins, and his one-night-a-week performances at Vaughan's Lounge.

Hear Dat is not meant to compete with the breadth or depth of these other books. I am far from a music authority. My last gig was searching for the notes of "Twinkle, Twinkle, Little Star" on a plastic flutophone in the third grade. A room full of tone-deaf 9-year-olds were taught by the patient and perhaps hard of hearing Mr. Kaczmarsky. We called him Mr. K.

This book is intended for the visitor or local looking to get a broad sense but not an indoctrination of our music, where it comes from and where to go tonight.

While widely recognized as the birthplace of Jazz, New Orleans is likewise an essential sweet spot for blues, gospel, R&B, zydeco, and Cajun music, and is the home of both brass band and bounce music. There'd be no funk without The Meters of New Orleans. And record labels No Limit Records and Lil Wayne's Cash Money Records were and are pivotal in the emergence of hip hop.

There is, unquestionably a New Orleans sound. If you're having a hard time identifying it, use Google or YouTube to search for songs you know very well, like "Sweet Dreams" by the Eurythmics or The Rolling Stones's "Gimme Shelter." Then bring up cover versions by New Orleans bands (Soul Rebels and Galactic, respectively) and as soon as the brass section comes in to join the distinctive loose, basic downbeat-backbeat of the drums, you'll experience your *aha* moment.

As is the case with everything in or about New Orleans, our musical history is likewise awash in story. Jazz, born on Congo Square, set its roots and grew into an international art form from the lobbies of the brothels of Storyville. The word *jazz* itself is said to have come from the jasmine perfume that most of the prostitutes wore. After a gentleman partook of these services in Storyville, their friends or business chums would often say, "Man, you smell like you just got jazzed."

Hear Dat offers no sexual favors, not even mere verbal titillation (unless you find the word *tresillo* sexy as all get out). But it is my hope the words on these pages will seduce you to plunge into New Orleans and "dance yo ass off" in the most historic and richest music scene in America.

Phtotographs in the Carol M. Highsmith Archive, Library of Congress, Prints and Photographs Division

DISCLAIMER

In my first book, *Eat Dat*, I had to leave out restaurants. I wrote profiles of only 250 of our 1,400. In my last book, *Fear Dat*, our way-too-many ghost stories were cut down to less than 10. However, here it felt like cruel and unusual banishment to leave out individual or groups of musicians. I apologize upfront to Valerie Sassyfras, Alexis & the Samurai, Antoine Diel Trio, and Chicken & Waffles, whose only mention in this book you just read.

Before you post mean tweets or inflict the public humiliation of one-star reviews on Amazon or Goodreads, do know there are many artists not included here who I have paid money to see and will do so again. The demands of a book simply require that some first-rate musicians will hit the cutting room floor.

OVERTURE WITH ALLEN TOUSSAINT

New Orleans is home to countless great musicians. This entire book could be filled front to back by merely listing their names, Alvin Alcorn to Linnzi Zaorski, without using a single adjective or verb. There are far fewer musicians who can be considered icons. Louis Armstrong and Professor Longhair should be on everyone's list. Jelly Roll Morton, Buddy Bolden, Fats Domino, and Danny Barker should certainly be considered. Ernie K-Doe fervently made his own case. Allen Toussaint would likewise be on anyone's list of icons.

Since *The Wild Sounds of New Orleans,* his debut album in 1958, Allen Toussaint has been involved in every aspect of the music business: producer, arranger, songwriter, talent scout, and, of course, singer and performer. One of the songs from his debut album, *Java,* became a #4 hit on the Billboard charts when covered by Al Hirt. This gave Mr. Toussaint his first taste of royalties. When combined with the weariness he experienced while performing one-night stands as part of Shirley & Lee's road band, he was convinced he'd be happier focusing on studio work and staying back home in New Orleans.

In 1960, he joined Minit Records, where he wrote and produced a number of hit songs including the first #1 song ever recorded in New Orleans, Ernie K-Doe's "Mother-in-Law." He likewise helped Irma Thomas's career with hit songs, "It's Raining" and "Ruler of My Heart," Chris Kenner's "I Like It Like That," "Down Home Girl" by Alvin Robinson, Benny Spellman's "Fortune Teller" and "Lipstick Traces," "Get Out of My Life, Woman" for Lee Dorsey, and Aaron Neville's "Hercules."

Toussaint has been a key figure in every major development in New Orleans music over the past 50-plus years, be it R&B, soul, or funk. He's in the Rock and Roll Hall of Fame. He has worked with major performers including Lee Dorsey, Dr. John, The Meters, the Pointer Sisters, Aaron Neville, Solomon Burke, Patti LaBelle, Cyndi Lauper, Paul Simon, Lenny Kravitz, even Paul McCartney, and more recently Elvis Costello and Eric Clapton.

His songs have been covered by The Rolling Stones ("Fortune Teller"); The Doors ("Get Out of My Life, Woman"); Devo ("Working in a Coal Mine"); Boz Scaggs; Robert Palmer; and hip hop stars, ODB, Biz Markie, KRS-One, and Outkast. Glenn Campbell took Toussaint's song "Southern Nights" to the top of the country and pop charts.

In 2013, Toussaint was awarded the National Medal of Arts. President Obama praised him while presenting the honor, saying, "Mr. Toussaint has built a legendary career alongside America's finest musicians, sustaining his city's rich tradition of rhythm and blues and lifting it to the national stage."

In spite of his immense and sweeping success and his universal high regard, Allen Toussaint remained reticent to talk about himself. He has said, "I'm not accustomed to talking about myself. I talk in the studio with musicians, or through my songs."

To that end, rather than making him painfully script a self-focused introduction, I offered Mr. Toussaint the opportunity to improvise, to issue spontaneous responses to quotes from others.*

If you asked me what kind of food we serve in New Orleans, I'd say we serve New Orleans food. —Emeril Lagasse

 How would you describe the kind of music we play in New Orleans?
The music of New Orleans has a rumba, Caribbean, and Indian frenzy all intertwined together that makes for an interesting combination of sounds. It is a music unique to this city and I feel the richest anywhere in the world.

New Orleans is the only place I know of where you ask a little kid what he wants to be and instead of saying, I want to be a policeman, or I want to be a fireman, he says, I want to be a musician. —Allan Jaffe

 How did growing up in Gert Town shape your musical aspirations?
I was surrounded by wonderful part-time musicians and various aspiring artists. The older guys used to get together and want to jam, and I was eager to listen and learn everything I was hearing. Just hanging out was like getting a degree from Julliard.

If I had grown up in any place but New Orleans, I don't think my career would have taken off. I wouldn't have heard the music that was around this town. —Pete Fountain

 Which musician, or song, or movement most influenced your music?
No one influenced my music more than Professor Longhair. I had many wonderful musical life teachers but when I heard Professor Longhair I heard everything I needed to hear and I immersed myself in his playing and his style. I had been playing the boogie-woogies and the shuffles as I heard them on radio and on some records. Then I heard Professor Longhair with this stuff that wasn't like anything else. He was dancing to a different drummer. When I heard Professor Longhair, that really stomped on my life. I didn't want to play "like" him. I wanted to be him.

Then there was a gentleman named Ernest Penn who came through my life when I was about age 12. He used to be a banjo player during the jitney days in New Orleans. He came from the era that if you played a string instrument you played everything that had a string on it. So he played banjo, mandolin, violin, bass, piano. Ernest Penn introduced me to stride piano style, which enlarged the piano and my entire musical scope.

By the time I met him, his gigging days were over, he had no instrument, and he had come from off the scene to live out his days with either his aunt or grandmother.

He heard me playing the piano in my house one day. When I came out, he introduced himself: "I play everything with a string on it and I was a master banjo player." He was a very spicy man with no teeth. My parents hated him. My mother especially didn't want him around because he smelled strongly of alcohol all the time. I would set on the porch every morning, waiting till he'd wake up and bring him over to the house to play and show me some of this butterfly technique and these old songs. He would play things like "High Society."

He was very patient with me with this kind of music because there was so much going on. He would slow it down for me to see what it was. He added tenths into my left hand—he added tenths into my whole life.

Jazz is alive, it's not a cannon ball. —Sunpie Barnes

 Where do you see New Orleans music evolving? And is this a good thing, a bad thing, or a let's-wait-and-see thing?
New Orleans music is constantly evolving into wonderful avenues. We have great ambassadors out in the world in every genre of music from rap to traditional to modern jazz and it continues to grow. The young cats like Troy Andrews, Harry Connick Jr., and Jonathan Batiste are representing the city in fine fashion.

To get to New Orleans you don't pass through anywhere else.

—Allen Toussaint

 Ending on your own quotation, please expand on what you fully meant here. And, having nearly lost New Orleans in 2005, why is it so important the city remains alive and vibrant?
Geographically speaking you don't have to pass through anyplace else to arrive in N.O. Anyone coming to New Orleans didn't get here trying to get to someplace else; they were coming to the city. New Orleans has richness and a charm

about it that no other place in the world can duplicate. The feel and flow of the Mississippi River and the warmth of the people make the city what it is, and that is worth saving. People in New Orleans are not always rich in finances but they are rich in culture, tradition, spirit, and history.

---

*Mere months after agreeing to participate in *Hear Dat* and after my original manuscript had been delivered to my publisher with this Q&A, Allen Toussaint passed away on November 9, 2015, while on tour in Madrid. As always, he was spreading the gospel of New Orleans music. He was not only a great musician, but a great ambassador for New Orleans, and an unfailingly great and generous man.

Allen Toussaint said in a 2013 interview on WWL-TV, "Everyday life is inspirational, if you're just open to it and enjoy the scenes and the interaction of people as they interact with each other. There are new things being performed every day if you just look around and enjoy what's happening, you'll never run out of inspiration."

CHAPTER 1

Jazz

If you have to ask what jazz is, you'll never know. —**Louis Armstrong**

Long ago, dinosaurs ruled the earth. (I didn't want to open this book with the overused phrase "New Orleans is the birthplace of jazz," and so I chose to write another thing you've likewise read or heard a thousand times.)

How jazz was birthed at Congo Square is a story you've probably read only a few hundred times. But since 27 percent of Americans think Neil Armstrong's walk on the moon was a hoax and more than 50 percent of Congress think climate change is a myth created by godless scientists, I sense stating the obvious may be shocking to many.

How America was settled by the British leaving their home country to sail across the ocean in rickety wooden boats where they sought religious freedom is a well-worn story. Not so here in New Orleans. La Louisiane (named for Louis XIV of France) became a colony of the Kingdom of France in 1682, was passed to Spain in 1763, and passed back to France in 1800, only to be sold to the United States in 1803. (Sort of a historical double reverse or flea flicker play.) This simple timeline of our history may anger the descendants of the Tchefuncte, Plaquemine, and Caddoan cultures, who predate any Europeans by as much as a thousand years.

The fact that we were a French-Spanish-French settlement and not one run by those freedom-seeking Brits means everything to jazz history. Here, through *Code noir*, the slaves were given Sundays off and allowed to congregate in public places, such as along the levees, public squares, or large backyards where they would sing, dance, play music, and practice voodoo from their West African or Haitian homelands. Elsewhere in America, those freedom-seeking Brits would never allow anything but proper Christian hymns and prayers on Sunday. Slaves up North were sometimes given a pound of salted cod on the holy day instead.

In 1817, or 14 years after the United States took over control of New Orleans, Mayor Macarty issued an ordinance that restricted slave gatherings to one single

Congo Square   Creative Commons /Bart Everson

location placed at the back of town. Place des Nègres, informally known as Congo Square, was officially and ridiculously changed to Beauregard Square, after New Orleans's Civil War general P. G. T. Beauregard. This name stood from 1893 until 2011, when the city changed the name back to what most everyone was still calling it, Congo Square. The only positive aspect of Macarty's restrictions is that we now know exactly where jazz was born. Well, that, and also that Congo Square became a boon for New Orleans, drawing numerous tourists and their dollars to hear the unique bamboulas and banzas playing on the square.

New Orleans jazz combines brass band marches, French quadrilles, beguine, ragtime, and blues—all upon a foundation of African traditions using a single-line melody and call-and-response pattern, with the rhythms of a counter-metric structure. Jazz purists, or even jazz know-a-little-bit-ists, will probably cringe at my attempt to define the music. Jazz is considered difficult to define, even for "experts." Ella Fitzgerald and Mel Tormé once attempted to define it in a speech they gave at the 1976 Grammy Awards. Theirs was a three-minute scat classic without a single "real" word.

The one constant and key element of jazz is improvisation. Said saxophonist, J. J. Johnson, "Jazz is restless. It won't stay put and it never will."

As jazz spread from New Orleans, it evolved different regional and local musical styles. By the 1930s, Kansas City-style jazz was heavily arranged dance-oriented swing band music. Gypsy jazz, a style that emphasized musette waltzes, had become popular up North. Bebop emerged in the 1940s and shifted jazz from dance music toward a challenging "musician's music," which was played at faster tempos and used more chord-based improvisation. Cool jazz introduced smoother sounds and long, linear melodic lines that you'd associate with clubs teeming with black turtlenecks, cigarette smoke, and angst-ridden poetry. Jazz today is . . . well . . . jazz.

Buddy, Bunk, King, Kid, Jelly Roll, and Pops: The Founding Fathers of Jazz

Serving as the New Orleans version of George Washington, Thomas Jefferson, and Benjamin Franklin, the founding fathers of jazz include Charles Joseph "Buddy" Bolden, Joseph Nathan "King" Oliver, Jelly Roll Morton, Edward "Kid" Ory, Willie Geary "Bunk" Johnson, and, most famously, Louis Armstrong, nicknamed both Satchmo and Pops (and once in a while Dipper).

Buddy Bolden

Buddy Bolden, born 1877, is credited by many as the Father of Jazz. He played the cornet strictly by ear and in a music style that merged marching band music, black spiritual, and rural blues. He was known for his improvised, wide open, and intensely loud playing. Before performing, Buddy would blast his signature "call his children home" riff so folks across town could hear he was about to unleash a raucous set. Most important, he is said to have invented the so-called

Monument to Buddy Bolden

"Big Four." Contemporary jazz great, Wynton Marsalis describes it "The Big Four was the first syncopated bass drum pattern to deviate from the standard on-the-beat march. The second half of the Big Four is a pattern commonly known as the habanera rhythm, one of the most basic rhythmic cells in Afro-Latin music traditions."

More than using new technique, Buddy Bolden captured a young audience with his revolutionary raunchy lyrics, delivered in Buddy's reportedly guttural moan. Consider Buddy's band the 2 Live Crew or Lil Wayne of their day, except of course Buddy was hugely more innovative and historically more important. The band would squeeze overflowing crowds into funky, rough roadhouse places like the Union Sons Hall on Perdido Street and they'd often play on until 5:00 a.m.

Some of their songs, like "Careless Love" and "My Bucket's Got a Hole in It," remain standards to this day. "Funky Butt," also called "Buddy Bolden's Blues," became their signature song. The well-known song was so off color, even whistling the melody in public was considered offensive.

Bolden, always a heavy drinker, suffered episodes of acute alcoholic psychosis and was given a diagnosis of dementia at the young age of 30. He spent the last 24 years of his life in the Louisiana State Insane Asylum. He was buried in Holt Cemetery, a potter's field, at the edge of New Orleans. There are two plaques inside Holt honoring the Father of Jazz, but no definitive gravesite. There are likewise no known recordings of Buddy Bolden's band. Trombonist Willy Cornish recalls that the band made a phonograph cylinder in the late 1890s, but none have ever been found.

King Oliver

King Oliver may not have been the Father of Jazz, but as written by one of his disciples, Louis Armstrong, "I still think that if it had not been for Joe Oliver, jazz would not be what it is today."

Oliver started out playing the cornet and then switched to trumpet. But his most lasting legacy is that of composer. His songs "Dippermouth Blues," "Sweet Like This," "Canal Street Blues," and "Doctor Jazz" remain jazz standards. He also inventively stretched the sounds performers could get from a trumpet with his pioneering use of mutes. He used plumbers' rubber plungers, bowler hats, bottles, cups, and his favorite, a small metal mute made by the company C. G. Conn. Conn, a grocery store owner, baker, and amateur cornet player, started making horn mouthpieces and accessories after a bar fight split his lip so badly that he was unable to play.

Unlike Buddy Bolden, Oliver's band crossed racial lines. His music was popular in both black dance halls in Storyville's red-light district as well as at white society debutant balls.

Sadly, like Bolden, at the end of his life Oliver also experienced many misfortunes. A series of managers stole money from him. Trying to negotiate a deal without a manager, he lost inking a contract with the Cotton Club in New York City by asking for too much. The job went to a young and then-little-known Duke Ellington.

A passion for sugar sandwiches led to pyorrhea and other gum diseases, leaving King Oliver unable to play. Broke, he pawned his trumpets and the suits he wore for performances, and ended up working odd jobs at a fruit stand and as a janitor. He died at age 57, unable to afford treatment for arteriosclerosis.

Jelly Roll Morton

Jelly Roll Morton, born Ferdinand Lamothe in 1890, grew up in New Orleans and started to learn piano at the age of 10. Two years later, he was working in the bordellos of Storyville, playing ragtime, French quadrilles, and other popular dance songs. By 14, Jelly Roll was working a Southern circuit, playing in many cities in Louisiana, Mississippi, Alabama, and Florida. He apparently also picked up a passion for gambling and pool playing. While New Orleans remained his base, his road life expanded to Memphis, St. Louis, and Kansas City, frequently working in minstrel shows.

Morton uniquely fused a variety of black musical styles: ragtime, vocal and instrumental blues, minstrel show tunes, field and levee hollers, religious hymns, spirituals, plus hints of Caribbean music. He created a musical gumbo that was just then beginning to be called "jazz."

By 1926, Morton was recording with his Red Hot Peppers, an eight-piece band organized to record the New Orleans-style music. The recordings were a perfect blend of adept composition and inventive improvisation. Cuts like "Grandpa's Spells," "Black Bottom Stomp," and "The Pearls" are masterly examples of Morton's immense talents as a composer, arranger, and on-of-a-kind pianist.

Like so many of the early jazz musicians, hard times visited Jelly Roll. His brand of music went out of style, replaced by the swing and big band era. He ended up managing and only occasionally playing at a dive bar in Washington, DC. During this time, he poetically lost the imbedded diamond that gleamed from the front tooth in his ever-ready smile.

In 1938, Jelly Roll was "discovered" by Alan Lomax who recorded him in a series of interviews about early jazz for the Library of Congress. In this invaluable oral history, Morton recalled in words and performances his early days in New Orleans. The Library of Congress recordings rekindled public interest in Morton's career and helped lead to a New Orleans music revival.

Unfortunately, Jelly Roll died just before the full Dixieland revival that rescued so many of his fellow musicians from obscurity. He blamed his declining health on a voodoo spell.

Kid Ory

Kid Ory was the original "tailgate" trombonist, a revolutionary style where the trombone plays a rhythmic line underneath the trumpets and cornets. His enormous brassy sound, newfangled sliding style of playing (glissandi), and his big personality and loud sense of humor came to define the New Orleans trombone sound, a style that continues to this day with Trombone Shorty, Corey Henry, and Lucien Barbarin.

A virtual prodigy, he was chosen to play in Buddy Bolden's band when he was only 13 years old, but his parents felt he was too young. After his 21st birthday, Ory left home to start his music career in New Orleans. He formed a small band that performed mostly in Lincoln and National Parks. The band went on to become one of the most successful in New Orleans.

Ory composed many early day jazz hits, including "Ory's Creole Trombone" and "Muskrat Ramble." Most significantly, in 1922, he made a historic set of recordings in Los Angeles. Under the pseudonym "Spikes Seven Pods of Pepper Orchestra," the records were the first ever by an African American jazz group.

Financially mismanaged by bandleader Freddie Washington, Kid Ory chose to leave the music business. He ran a chicken farm for nearly 10 years. In the late 1930s, a revival of interest in old-time jazz brought him back to the stage and recording studio. He convinced fellow Dixieland-era musicians to join his new band, the Hot Five. They recorded jazz classics like "Heebie Jeebies," "Savoy Blues," "Hotter Than That," and "I'm Not Rough." The song "Struttin' With Some Barbecue" features a Kid Ory solo that typifies his style, and it is still played most every week as a standard in sets by Kermit Ruffins & the Barbecue Swingers. Getting a major breakthrough, Kid's band got regular work on Orson Welles's nationwide radio broadcasts, and he began playing again for packed halls.

Fans of the then-new bebop jazz criticized his Dixieland style as "moldly figs." Ory rose above it and refused to respond in kind. He said in a *DownBeat* magazine interview: "I don't condemn any style of music. I love to see any style go over."

William P. Gottlieb, Library of Congress

Bunk Johnson

Willie Geary Johnson was born in either 1879 or 1889. An uncovered census shows his birth as the latter. He claimed the former to back up his assertion that he played in Buddy Bolden's band and wasn't wearing diapers at the time. He also claimed to have taught a young Louis Armstrong everything he knows. Armstrong himself refuted that boast and said King Oliver was his mentor. These disputed statements, and many others, is how he got his nickname, Bunk.

What is true is that Bunk was an early pioneer for jazz and an exceptional cornet player. After being a regular member of The Superior Orchestra, he later joined the famous Eagle Band. His greatest contributions to jazz came later in life, in the 1940s. By the mid-1930s, Bunk had lost his teeth and was unable to perform. He worked in the sugar cane fields and other odd jobs to pay the rent. On the verifiable date of September 27, 1938, his life changed when he attended a Louis Armstrong concert at the New Iberia Training School. Louis recognized the down-on-his-luck old master and helped trigger a series of events that would get Bunk a new set of teeth, a new horn, a series of recording contracts, the first in 1942, and a revitalized career as a globe-trotting jazz man.

Bunk could play any type of jazz. His repertoire included ragtime, gospel, spirituals, marches, pop tunes, and jazz standards. He could play lyrically or rhythmically, soft as a whisper or gutbucket loud. He became critically important in the revitalization of jazz, not just for his playing, or for his spreading the gospel through long stints in San Francisco and New York with visits to Los Angeles, Boston, Chicago, and around the world, but also for his recorded interviews where he talked about New Orleans, his life, Buddy Bolden, funeral parades, and early jazz music. Bunk, in effect, laid down a permanent history of jazz. Bunk's influence and popularity was especially strong with European and Asian fans. Some say, and certainly Bunk would have agreed, that his legacy for New Orleans jazz overseas surpasses even that of Louis Armstrong. In Europe there is the Bunk Johnson Society and the Bunk Johnson Memorial Hospital.

Sidney Bechet

Sidney Bechet, a contemporary of Louis Armstrong, sadly has no nickname. We can make one up and call him "Shooter" for the incident in Paris when a woman was wounded during an exchange of gunfire that resulted in Bechet being jailed for nearly a year. The shootout started when another musician told Bechet that he was playing the wrong chord. Bechet challenged the man to a duel, saying, "Sidney Bechet never plays the wrong chord."

He was the undisputed king of the soprano saxophone, an instrument rarely played in jazz at that time. Bechet created a new and prominent place for the soprano sax as a solo instrument. His influence reaches, or has reached, countless musicians including John Coltrane, Wayne Shorter, and Branford Marsalis.

Duke Ellington said, "Bechet to me was the very epitome of jazz . . . everything he played his whole life was completely original. I honestly think he was the most unique man to ever be in this music."

Like Louis Armstrong and Kid Ory, Bechet was a child prodigy. By the age of 13, Bechet was a professional musician, much to his family's dismay. By 16, he was touring with pianist and singer Clarence Williams throughout the Deep South, later joining King Oliver's band in 1919 and traveling to Chicago, New York, and the jazz hubs in Europe.

Bechet co-led a group with pianist Willie "The Lion" Smith that recorded several early versions of what was later called Latin jazz, adapting traditional merengue, rumba, and Haitian songs to the jazz idiom, or an early version of what would become the New Orleans sound when reworked and shaped by Professor Longhair.

Unlike Armstrong, who had been a childhood friend growing up in New Orleans, Bechet never achieved great popularity in the United States. His music, however, has been more recently heard in the movies *Midnight in Paris,* directed by Woody Allen, the French film *Amélie,* and from Louis, the trumpet-playing gator in Disney's *The Princess and the Frog.*

Freddie Keppard

Freddie Keppard's career was sandwiched between Buddy Bolden (he was 13 years younger) and Louis Armstrong (11 years older). Playing with The Original Creole Orchestra, Freddie toured the vaudeville circuit, making the New Orleans style a sensation throughout the country.

He would probably be more famous today had he accepted the offer from the Victor Talking Machine Company to make the first jazz recordings. One reason this didn't happen was rumored to be that the Victor Company wanted him to tone down his too "hot" style to make the records more palatable (vanilla) for mainstream consumers. Sidney Bechet offered the more likely reason that Keppard was a casual "good time" guy, so prevalent in New Orleans then and now. He frankly had no interest in the deal. To him, the Victor Company represented big business and commercialization of the pure thing he loved. Had Keppard agreed to make recordings for them with the Original Creole Orchestra, he would have bastardized his pure enjoyment and turned it into a commodity.

Danny Barker

Danny Barker was not one of the founding fathers of jazz, but next generation. However, if I left him out of the jazz chapter, there's no doubt I would receive a rash of mean tweets. I probably will anyway for neglecting Billie and DeDe Pierce.

Danny Barker was a jazz banjoist, singer, guitarist, songwriter, and ukulele player. He played with Louis Armstrong, Fess Williams, Billy Fowler, the White Brothers, Buddy Harris, Albert Nicholas, Lucky Millinder, Benny Carter, Bunk Johnson, Dexter Gordon, Charlie Parker, Jelly Roll Morton, Baby Dodds, James P. Johnson, Sidney Bechet, Mezz Mezzrow, Red Allen, Ethel Waters, and Cab Calloway. In other words, everybody. After leaving Calloway, he started his own group that featured his wife Blue Lu Barker and the Fairview Baptist Church Brass Band. The band, renamed the Dirty Dozen Brass Band in later years, was pivotal in New Orleans jazz history, launching the careers of brothers Wynton

Marsalis and Branford Marsalis, Shannon Powell a.k.a. "The King of Treme," Lucien Barbarin, Dr. Michael White, Leroy Jones, and others. Joe Torregano, another Fairview band alumnus, said this: "That group saved jazz for a generation in New Orleans."

Beginning Bucket Bangers

Unlike rock drummers such as Keith Moon and Ginger Baker or later-day jazz drummers Max Roach and Buddy Rich, the early jazz drummers in the pre-Big Band era were not headliners and most are barely remembered. Louis "Old Man" Cottrell has been credited as the innovator of the press roll in jazz drumming and was indeed the most significant influence on generations of New Orleans drummers.

Adolphe Paul Barbarin and Warren "Baby" Dodds were born within six months of each other in New Orleans and are jointly regarded as the best drummers of the era. Barbarin had a classic education for a drummer, learning under Cottrell and touring first with King Oliver's band and then Louis Armstrong's. Baby Dodds, on the contrary, started playing in street parades. His break, playing in Kid Ory's band, turned into a nightmare when he was humiliated as all the musicians walked off stage because of his poor playing. This incident was like Michael Jordan being cut from his high school basketball team. It spurred him on to greatness.

Al Hirt and Pete Fountain: Pop Stars

Jazz purists might be annoyed that I include the hugely popular Al Hirt and Pete Fountain among consummate musicians like King Oliver and Sidney Bechet. Al Hirt was sometimes derided by critics and jazz purists for pandering to mass tastes. He often said himself that he was nothing more than a crowd-pleaser. "I'm a pop commercial musician. I never played jazz or improvised."

Early on in his career, Pete Fountain got his first national exposure as the clarinet player in the pathologically uncool Lawrence Welk and His Orchestra. Toward the end of his playing days, he had a club in the massive Hilton Riverside Hotel with its vapid convention-central décor that looks like it could be Anywhere, USA.

But these two music makers did more to make New Orleans–style jazz popular in Topeka and Pittsburgh than anyone else mentioned in this book.

Of his 55 recorded albums, Hirt placed 22 on the Billboard charts and won a Grammy Award in 1955. His album *Honey in the Horn* sold more than a million copies. Nicknamed Jumbo because of his size, Al Hirt was a genial host for New Orleans. He was seen all over town, in TV commercials and on billboards. He was also in several movies, was a minority owner of the city's NFL Saints team, and ran a popular club on Bourbon Street for 22 years until it closed in 1983.

Pete Fountain played the clarinet in jazz, Dixieland, honky-tonk, and pop styles. He was dismissed from the Lawrence Welk Show after he went improv and jazzed up the on-air rendition of "Silver Bells." Thereafter, he appeared a whopping 56 times on *The Tonight Show Starring Johnny Carson*. Fountain recorded more than 100 records, many in the Dixieland style, but others contained only a mere whiff of any type of jazz.

Pete, like his good friend Al Hirt, opened up a jazz club on Bourbon Street. It became a 1960s happenin' place that was frequented by Frank Sinatra, Robert Mitchum, Brenda Lee, Carol Lawrence, and Robert Goulet. He closed the club in 2003, but he continued to perform as a fixture in 44 Jazz Fests. He founded The Half-Fast Walking Club, one of the best-known marching krewes at Mardi Gras. The original name was The Half-Assed Walking Club and was meant to be a well-oiled (i.e., drunk) parade of musicians. The name was changed under considerable pressure by Mardi Gras organizers.

Pete Fountain, who is still alive as of this writing, retired from playing at age 83. His final set was on May 5, 2013, at Jazz Fest.

George Lewis

George Lewis is mostly just locally known, and his renown is based more upon his reach and influence than pure talent. Music historian Gary Giddins described Lewis as "an affecting musician with a fat-boned sound but limited technique."

He began playing professionally as a 17-year-old, working regularly with Buddy Petit and Chris Kelly as well as with the great Kid Ory. He took gigs when he could get them while he worked grinding hours as a wharf rat unloading ships.

In 1942, when a group of jazz enthusiasts came to New Orleans to record the old master, Bunk Johnson, Lewis was chosen to accompany him on the clarinet. Previously almost unknown outside of New Orleans, Lewis was then asked to make additional recordings to document the music of older New Orleans jazz musicians and bands. National tours soon followed with the group touted as "the last of the real New Orleans jazz bands." As a clarinet player with a great number of solos, to everyone's surprise (including his own), Lewis became a symbol of the New Orleans jazz tradition and one of the most popular figures of the jazz revival movement of the 1950s.

Louis Armstrong

Getting the last word is an honor that has to go to Louis Armstrong, but it won't be many words. Just as you already knew "New Orleans is the birthplace of Jazz," I assume most anyone picking up a book called *Hear Dat* can recite Satchmo's story: how he said he was born on the Fourth of July 1900, but it was actually August 4, 1901; how he was tossed into the New Orleans Colored Waifs Home after a run-in with the police; how upon hearing his extraordinary and yet untrained skills, King Oliver took him under his wing and taught him how to read music and work on his playing technique; and how he exceeded every other jazz musician before, during, and after his unparalleled career.

Louis Armstrong's importance cannot be overstated. He was an innovator of

A stylized rendering of Louis Armstrong   Mark Mestre

epic proportions. Armstrong's sense of rhythm and timing took jazz from a formal 2/4 beat to a languid, more sophisticated 4/4 feel. He completely redefined the context in which the trumpet was played, launching the instrument from a backup role to center stage. His talent as a singer, trumpeter, and composer and his showmanship brought worldwide attention to New Orleans jazz.

Pops's recordings in Chicago with the Hot Five, a group of first-rate musicians (most from New Orleans), are among the most important recordings in jazz history. The Hot Five sessions enabled Armstrong to create his own musical style, for the first time featuring his singing and talking. Emerging as the hanky-waving entertainer, he went on to become the official ambassador of music and goodwill, performing jazz throughout the world under sponsorship of the U.S. Department of State.

Based on my third-grade flutophone sophistication, I always liked Louis Armstrong's music. But it wasn't until I saw a film clip of jazz scholar Gary Giddins that I fully appreciated Satchmo's genius. Playing the opening cadenza of the song "West End Blues," Giddins explained what we hear basically cannot be done by a human being. Now, every time I hear it, I get all choked up.

CHAPTER 2

Getting a Wiggle On
(Where to Hear Live Jazz Tonight)

Jazz came out of New Orleans, and that was the forerunner of everything. You mix jazz with European rhythms, and that's rock 'n' roll, really. You can make the argument that it all started on the streets of New Orleans. —**The Edge**

Sadly, some jazz musicians worth your time and money will be left off these pages. Fortunately, an article on *The Huffington Post* comforted me that 20 percent of Americans read only one book a year. A whopping 28 percent don't read any books at all. While these statistics are utterly depressing for book people, they take the pressure off me to get it all down. Statistically, practically no one is reading this book and so I won't fret (too much) that deserving jazz artists like Christian Scott and Jerry Zigmont are not included here.

The Palm Court Jazz Café (1204 Decatur Street) doesn't have quite the history and reputation of Preservation Hall, but a venerable jazz orchestra along with their Creole cuisine is served up every Wednesday through Sunday, since 1989. Unfortunately, their headliner, trumpeter Lionel Ferbos, passed away in 2014. Up until a few weeks before his death, Mister Lionel sat in with the band every Friday night. He was 103 years old, at the time the world's oldest living jazz musician. When I spoke with a staff person at Palm Court, almost as if selling me, they offered, "We still have two 90-year-olds."

On their nighttime Mississippi River cruises, the Steamboat Natchez features the Grammy-nominated Dukes of Dixieland. The original band was formed in 1948 by Papa Jac Assunto and his sons Frank and Fred, and later Bob (a.k.a. Duke). The band ended its affiliation with the Assunto family in the mid-1970s, but has since recorded CDs (*Gloryland* was the Grammy nominee), collaborated with The Oak Ridge Boys (*When Country Meets Dixie*), and has performed in more than 30 venues worldwide, including Carnegie Hall in New York.

Venue Highlight

PRESERVATION HALL
726 St. Peter St.
Phone: 504-522-2481

For those who come to New Orleans and want to hear the New Orleans jazz that's most often thought of as New Orleans jazz, Preservation Hall is hallowed ground. Located in the heart of the French Quarter, a block behind Jackson Square, right next to Pat O'Brien's and directly across the street from Reverend Zombie's House of Voodoo. I give all these landmarks because Preservation Hall's sign (too highly hung and too-discreet old gold letters on black backing) is easy to miss. This intimate venue has been playing three shows a night, at 8:15, 9:15, and 10:15, 350 days a year, since 1961. Preservation Hall easily draws in more listeners than any music club in New Orleans.

Preservation Hall

The space was previously an art gallery where owner Larry Borenstein had the bright idea to have noted jazz musicians perform inside his space. His goals were to draw in customers and to also allow him to hear the music he loved, but had few chances to hear because he was continuously strapped to running the gallery.

In 1960, a newly married couple from Pennsylvania, Allan and Sandra Jaffe, passed through New Orleans on the way back from their honeymoon. During their intended short visit they heard about "Mr. Larry's Gallery." Going there, the Jaffes were seduced, I mean seduced to the point of picking up roots in Pennsylvania, moving to New Orleans, buying the gallery space, and converting it into the now-famous jazz hall.

In his passion to preserve the old-time music, Allan Jaffe organized the Preservation Hall Jazz Band for performances both in his space and he set up a series of performances in the Midwest to spread the gospel. Fifty-five years later, now under the leadership of the Jaffes' son Ben, the performances remain today as they ever were. Inside there is no food, no drinks, no bathrooms, no air conditioning, and for late arrivals, there aren't even any seats. You just sit (and some nights sweat) on the floor. For the 45-minute session, it's just you and the musicians, playing at arm's length in an intimate and moving experience of live acoustic jazz performed by masters. The band actually has many members to allow nightly performances in New Orleans as well as more than 100 tour dates worldwide, now spreading the gospel as far as Japan.

Preservation Hall holds to their mission to broaden awareness of traditional New Orleans Jazz through recordings, multimedia projects, maintenance of an archive of New Orleans music, and, more recently, collaborations of their traditional jazz joined by noted performers of other styles. Dave Grohl and the Foo Fighters did a session there with jazz band members for their new album and HBO series, *Sonic Highways*. The Preservation Hall band has also recorded with Blind Boys of Alabama, My Morning Jacket, Pete Seeger, Tom Waits, Mos Def, Lenny Kravitz, and The Edge from U2. It isn't likely Lenny Kravitz or The Edge will be sitting in on a night you go, but there will always be a headline performer like Leroy Jones, Lucien Barbarin, and Shannon Powell, musicians you may not know—but should.

Said Louis Armstrong, "Preservation Hall. Now that's where you'll find all of the greats."

Trombone Shorty

As far as individual performers go, Troy "Trombone Shorty" Andrews would be at or near the top of a must-see list, except he rarely plays in New Orleans anymore. For the first half of 2016, he has 30 scheduled dates, performing in Pittsburgh, Dallas, Atlanta, Miami, Nashville, with others in Italy, Germany, Japan, Poland, Austria, France, Spain, and Mexico. However, he does attend and play during most every Jazz & Heritage Festival.

Trombone Shorty began playing at the age of 6. He got his nickname parading with a second line and enthusiastically blowing a trombone said to be longer than he was tall. Andrews toured internationally for the first time at age 12 before joining Lenny Kravitz's horn section at the age of 19. His album *Backatown* received a Grammy nomination in 2011. The next CD, *For True*, topped *Billboard* magazine's contemporary jazz chart for 12 weeks. His more recent music has blended jazz with funk and hip hop to create a style he calls "Supafunkrock."

Josh Brasted

Kermit Ruffins

Kermit Ruffins is New Orleans jazz royalty who can actually be heard in New Orleans several times each week. He plays regularly at Blue Nile, Little Gem Saloon, Bullet's Sports Bar, occasionally the Rock 'n' Bowl, and twice a week at his own Kermit's Mother-in-Law Lounge. Until 2013, Thursday nights at Vaughan's was a nearly iconic event. For 20 years, Ruffins and his band, the Barbecue Swingers, would pack the Bywater joint tighter than two coats of paint. Ruffins simply felt it was time to move on.

He began his professional career as a founding member in the Rebirth Brass Band back when he was still in high school. Early on, the teenage musicians would busk the French Quarter streets, playing for tip money. Young, inexperienced, but talented, they soon were picked to be the house band at the Glass House, a tiny club with a great musical heritage in a tough section of South Saratoga Street. The Rebirth Brass Band released seven critically acclaimed records and began playing around the world. By the time they won the Grammy Award for their 2011 CD release, *Rebirth of New Orleans*, Ruffins had long since left the band and had done so as amicably as he left Vaughan's.

In 1992, Ruffins set off on a career that dropped brass band and focused on his passion for classic New Orleans jazz. His new quintet was named the Barbecue Swingers because of Ruffins's practice of firing up the grill in the bed of his pickup truck before the band played. By the end of the first set, the barbecue was ready.

Beyond his virtuoso trumpet playing (or cooking) skills, Ruffins, in many ways embodies the spirit of New Orleans music. Like his hero, Louis Armstrong, he's free spirited, swinging, and always with a ready smile. Ruffins performs in his signature fedora, sometimes with a bandana tied underneath. When I saw him one year at French Quarter Festival, Ruffins closed his set with the comment, "This was the first time I've played straight in I don't know how many years."

Like Louis Armstrong, Ruffins's importance to New Orleans jazz cannot be overstated, as he helped keep it alive by bringing jazz to younger and hipper audiences.

The Marsalis Clan

The Marsalis Family is the unofficial first family of jazz. Patriarch Ellis Marsalis, the great pianist and teacher, helped to raise four noted musicians: saxophonist Branford, trumpeter and composer Wynton, trombonist Delfeayo, and drummer Jason.

Ellis was a cofounder of AFO (All For One) Records, one of America's first independent, black-owned record companies. He was, at that time, one of the few New Orleans musicians just not that into New Orleans Dixieland or rhythm and blues. Instead, he played the more sophisticated hard bop and modernist jazz.

Though he has recorded almost 20 of his own albums, and was featured on many others, Ellis stepped just to the side of the spotlight to focus on his teaching. He is currently affiliated with the Jazz Studies program at the University of New Orleans. His music teaching style encourages students to make discoveries on their own, through experimentation and very careful listening. Ellis has influenced the careers of countless musicians, including Terence Blanchard, Harry Connick Jr., Nicholas Payton, and, of course, his four sons.

The Ellis Marsalis Center for Music in the Upper Ninth Ward is a premier and infinitely affordable educational center. To keep our music traditions alive and to ensure they are passed on to the next generation, lessons are taught by first-class musicians and cost next to nothing. My daughter took an entire term of classes on the stand-up bass for only $30.

The Ellis Marsalis Quartet plays most Friday nights at Snug Harbor on Frenchmen Street.

Son and revered trumpeter, Wynton Marsalis, is less often seen and heard in New Orleans these days. He has won Grammy Awards in both jazz and classical music, won the Pulitzer Prize, and was practically the full-time narrator for Ken Burns's documentary on jazz. He is now the artistic director for jazz at Lincoln Center in New York.

Saxophonist son, Branford, has two Grammy Awards of his own and runs an independent record label, Marsalis Music. Growing up, he had the age-appropriate disdain for his father's taste in music, preferring James Brown and Elton John over Miles Davis and John Coltrane. (Growing up, I also rolled my eyes every time my father popped Les Baxter or Robert Goulet on the record console.) Brandon later admitted in an interview in *JazzTimes* magazine his dislike for jazz was a maturity thing. "Jazz is not for kids," he notes. "Jazz has a level of sophistication that's just too hip for kids." He went on to be the bandleader for *The Tonight Show with Jay Leno,* and he has performed with Sting, the Grateful Dead, and Bruce Hornsby.

Gifted trombonist Delfeayo has played on fewer albums than his father or siblings, but is a prolific producer of acoustic jazz recordings. He's made more than 100 recordings for others, including Harry Connick Jr., Terence Blanchard, his brothers

Branford and Wynton, father Ellis, and many more. He also founded the Uptown Music Theatre. His theater has trained more than 300 youths and has staged eight original musicals. As a trombonist, Delfeayo has toured with Ray Charles, Art Blakey's Jazz Messengers, and Abdullah Ibrahim. He currently plays with his own Delfeayo Marsalis Sextet and the Uptown Jazz Orchestra, a group he formed in 2008 that features 16 players. His mission with the jazz orchestra is to be able to play music from the early 1900s to now. He takes on the responsibility to do his part to continue the legacy of what he called in an interview in the *New Orleans Advocate* newspaper, "That groove, that thing that you can't describe, that's what people love about New Orleans music."

Youngest son Jason is fond of retelling his introduction to music: "When I was 3, my parents bought me a toy drum set and they used to introduce me to an imaginary audience. They would say, 'Ladies and gentleman introducing the fabulous Jason!' and I would come out and start banging away much to my parents' delight." By age 6, Jason had his first real drum set and was also taking lessons from the legendary New Orleans drummer James Black. At age 7 he was sitting in with his father's jazz group. He was starting to become a seasoned road veteran before the age of 9.

Talented in all drumming styles, Jason has played straight-ahead jazz with Dr. Michael White, jazz fusion (Neslort), Brazilian jazz (Casa Samba), even Celtic music; and his most successful group, the Latin-sounding Los Hombres Calientes.

The entire Marsalis family of musicians won the 2011 Jazz Master Fellowship Awards from the National Endowment for the Arts. It is the highest honor that the United States bestows upon jazz musicians.

Leroy Jones

Leroy Jones, like the Marsalis family, is a contemporary missionary for New Orleans traditional jazz. He has been called the "keeper of the flame," and critics consider him one of most technically talented musicians produced by New Orleans (and that is saying a lot). Jones has said his quintet seeks "to expose audiences everywhere to the authentic music of New Orleans, the music of Louis Armstrong, Buddy Bolden, Danny Barker, and all the other greats who have helped create the rich gumbo that is the sound of New Orleans."

He began performing at age 12 with the seminal Fairview Baptist Church Brass Band, widely credited with restoring interest in the brass band tradition. Jones went on to become a featured performer with Harry Connick Jr. and His Orchestra, where his playing and singing made him a crowd favorite. His TV appearances include *The Tonight Show, Good Morning America, Late Night with David Letterman, The Today Show, Arsenio Hall, Conan O'Brien,* and *Oprah Winfrey.*

Sometimes Leroy Jones sits in with Palm Court Jazz Café orchestra, he often joins the Preservation Hall Jazz Band, and he is a featured performer at most music festivals from the Jazz & Heritage Festival and Satchmo SummerFest, to the Tremé Festival.

Dr. Michael White

Sometimes it seems New Orleans jazz has more advocates than Jesus had apostles. Dr. Michael White is yet another gifted musician who doubles as a missionary for traditional jazz. Appearing on WGNO, he remembered that as a kid, "There was a time when I bought a George Lewis record and I put it on, and it was like a light came on and my whole life changed forever. It was like I instantly started to see and understand what it felt like to be from New Orleans."

The Doctor is not his nickname, but denotes his PhD. He has taught jazz history (and Spanish) for more than 25 years. Dr. White currently teaches African American music at Xavier University of Louisiana and holds an Endowed Chair in the Humanities of New Orleans Music and Culture.

White, a clarinetist, is a classically trained musician who began his jazz musical career as a teenager playing for Doc Paulin's Brass Band. He was thereafter a member of the Fairview Baptist Church Marching Band, established by Danny Barker. White founded the Liberty Brass Band in 1981 to preserve traditional brass band performance. He's played with the Young Tuxedo Brass Band since 1979, including a tribute to Jelly Roll Morton that was performed at Lincoln Center in 1989. He plays an end-of-year concert at the Village Vanguard in New York, which he has done every year since the early 1990s.

Locally, Dr. White can be heard on rare occasion at Little Gem Saloon and more often at Snug Harbor.

Shannon Powell

Powell is a modern-day Adolphe Paul Barbarin or Warren "Baby" Dodds, two drummers you probably didn't know before reading Chapter 1. Along with Stanton Moore, Powell is considered the city's premier drummer. He is nicknamed The King of Tremé, which honors both Powell and the intensely musical neighborhood where he grew up. He is also considered a leading force on the traditional jazz circuit and serves as a jazz educator and clinician. Powell has delivered workshops at universities and jazz festivals all over the world.

Like so many, he started very young. By age 6, Powell was playing drums regularly for his church, the First Garden Christ Church. Soon after, he began visiting and performing at Preservation Hall alongside local legends, such as Cié Frasier and Freddie Coleman.

Powell met Danny Barker while in elementary school. Barker chose Powell for his legendary Fairview Baptist Brass Band. Within a few years, Powell became a regular member of Barker's band and played professionally with Danny Barker & His Original Jazz Hounds. For five years, Powell toured extensively with Harry Connick Jr. and released two platinum albums with Connick.

Local pianist David Torkanowsky called Powell "living history. He's the last of his kind. This town is the beachhead of African culture in America, and he is a direct uncut descendant from that. I mean, the humidity is in his playing." NPR's John Burnett tabbed Shannon Powell "one of the greatest drummers this musical city has ever produced."

He can be heard, among other spots, every Tuesday night when he sits in with the Preservation Hall band, wearing his ever-present black beret and gap-toothed smile.

Tim Laughlin

Unlike Trombone Shorty and Shannon Powell who both started playing at the age of 6, Tim Laughlin waited until the ripe old age of 9 before he received his first clarinet and launched a musical career. He'd fallen in love with the sound of the clarinet, hearing it on the radio and listening to a childhood friend practicing.

Laughlin's style takes traditional Dixieland clarinet and improvises in ways that make it fresh and current for contemporary audiences. He's said, "The biggest delight is knowing I am continuing a great tradition of keeping a timeless art form alive. New Orleans is known for its great clarinetists, starting with Johnny Dodds, Jimmie Noone, Sidney Bechet, Albert Burbank, Irving Fazola, Eddie Miller, and Pete Fountain, as well. They were all known for their big sound and that's what perked my ears up when I was young."

He has recorded more than a dozen solo CDs, including *The Isle of Orleans* (2003), which garnered awards and showcased Laughlin as the first and only New Orleans clarinetist to ever write and record an entire album of originals.

He and Pete Fountain were the opening act when the legendary Blue Room in the Roosevelt Hotel reopened after renovations following Hurricane Katrina. You can catch Tim performing at his favorite clubs in New Orleans like the Palm Court, Richard Fiske's Martini Bar, Snug Harbor, and aboard the Steamboat Natchez.

Terrence Blanchard

Spike Lee movies, including *Do the Right Thing, Mo' Better Blues, Jungle Fever*, and *Malcolm X* have a distinctive sound. That sound is New Orleans native Terrence Blanchard. He has his own style of restrained, precise (I find it kind of beautifully haunting) modern jazz that has brought him a Grammy Award, countless scores for Hollywood movies, and fame, perhaps even more in the New York jazz scene than here in New Orleans.

Blanchard has absolutely developed his own style rather than mimicking Wynton Marsalis or other contemporary greats. He replaced Marsalis in Art Blakey's Jazz Messengers group in the 1980s, has played with Lionel Hampton, and now tours internationally.

Terence Blanchard doesn't play often in New Orleans anymore, but when he does . . . (such as the Voodoo Music + Arts Experience), he's totally worth your time and entrance fee.

Shamarr Allen

Shamarr Allen decided to play the trumpet at age 7 after his father played him a Louis Armstrong record. In the middle of some Herb Alpert and Pete Fountain, his dad popped Louis Armstrong on the turntable. Allen recalled in an interview with the *Times-Picayune* newspaper, "I was shocked. I was like, 'Dad, whatever he's playing, I want to play that.'"

His musical education was largely on the streets. Almost inevitably, he found himself playing on Jackson Square with Tuba Fats. "A lot of us learned a lot about traditional music from Tuba Fats," Allen says. "He would call a song, and I'd say, 'Tuba I don't know that one.' He'd say, 'Sink or swim, we're playing it. One, two . . .' You had to go home and learn it, and the next week when you came back, you had better be able to play it."

His own band, the Underdawgs, is a jazz band fighting not to be classified as such. They mix hip hop, jazz, funk, and rock. Singer and collaborator Paul Sanchez has called Allen a visionary, stating that he "takes New Orleans jazz into rock and pop in ways I haven't heard before." Allen classifies his music, "a bunch of jazz cats trying to play rock music, but now we've found our sound. We are the next thing from New Orleans."

He was chosen *OffBeat Magazine*'s best trumpet player for 2015. The group tours extensively and is often in unusual places like the Congo, Kazakhstan, Kyrgyzstan, and Turkmenistan. When in New Orleans, Allen can be heard at Tipitina's and at the large-venue festivals.

The Original Tuxedo Jazz Band

Not to be confused with the Original Dixieland Jazz Band, the Tuxedo Band, so named because of their attire and original location, started out as Storyville performers at the Tuxedo Dance Hall. The year was 1910 and the band was led by cornet player Oscar Phillip "Papa" Celestin. Other original members were George "Baba" Filhe, trombone; Peter Bocage, violin; Lorenzo Tio Jr., clarinet; T. Brouchard, bass; Manuel Manetta, piano; and Louis Cottrell, drums.

When legalized prostitution ended and the Storyville District was closed down, Papa and Baba took the Tuxedo Jazz Band out to perform at one-night club gigs, private dances, and society events. They became the darling of the New Orleans social scene in the 1920s. In 1953, they became the first jazz band to ever play at the White House. Who knew Dwight Eisenhower was so cool? More than 100 years after their start, you can still hear the currently assembled members of the Tuxedo Jazz Band every Monday night at Irvin Mayfield's club in the Royal Sonesta Hotel.

There is an entire book, *The Original Tuxedo Jazz Band*, written by Sally Newhart, where you can learn tons more than from these mere paragraphs.

Now, that other parvenu band, the Original Dixieland Jazz Band, didn't start up until 1917 (that is, seven years after the Tuxedo Band). Granted, they did make the first jazz recording, as well as 52 others between 1917 and 1936. Nick LaRocca, the original leader of the Original Dixieland Jazz Band, insisted they invented jazz, though few scholars would support that claim. But it is without question that the group played a major part in popularizing Dixieland jazz throughout America and Europe.

They stopped playing in 1936, or 80 years (and counting) before the Tuxedo Band.

Over Da River

There is a ferry at the base of Canal Street, near the aquarium, that crosses the Mississippi River to Algiers Point. Until recently, it was free. The ferry ride now costs $2.00. When visitors ask what there is to do at Algiers Point, the joking response is "Turn around and come back."

There are actually several restaurants and pubs on the point, as well as a ton of history. Algiers is the second oldest neighborhood in New Orleans after the French Quarter. In the 1800s, it was a hub of slaughterhouses and the slave trade.

By the early 1900s, Algiers had a lively music scene with 36 live venues and dance halls. Many

Old Point Bar

of the top musicians who played the newfangled jazz lived there, including Henry "Red" Allen, Peter Bocage, Oscar "Papa" Celestin, "Kid" Thomas Valentine, and Elizabeth "Memphis Minnie" Douglas. New Orleans residents and visitors flowed across the river to hear the new music on Algiers Point. Spending an evening there was commonly referred to as going "Over Da River."

The vast majority of the jazz venues have long since disappeared. Most of the saloons and dance halls are all but forgotten. There is, however, a Jazz Walk of Fame that honors 16 musicians, such as Sidney Bechet, Buddy Bolden, Danny Barker, Kid Ory, King Oliver, Jelly Roll Morton, and Louis Armstrong. Their glass-etched portraits were once illuminated at dusk and night by street lamps along the levee. Unfortunately, 13 of the 16 are damaged and will seemingly remain so while the National Recreation and Park Association argues with the city as to who should pay for repairs.

Creative Commons

The Old Point Bar is the one remaining music venue. There have been 40-some movies filmed using the bar because it looks like what Hollywood thinks a neighborhood bar should look like. Dated license plates are nailed to the wall and a kitschy collection of bobblehead dolls and an old military police sign are propped behind the bar. Its bartender, Patti Pujol, seems right out of central casting with her perpetual cowboy hat and an attitude that perfectly balances the line between sweet and smart-ass. Their small stage hosts some of the city's better musicians. Rick Trolsen draws large crowds Friday evenings. Amanda Walker, Romy Kaye, the Hill Country Hounds, and 12 Mile Limit are regulars.

Timothy Bulone

CHAPTER 3

Blues

*Only a black man have the blues. White man never
have the blues, he only feels bad.*   —Champion Jack Dupree

The blues did not originate in New Orleans. Rather, it emerged all across the Deep South at the end of the 19th century. If you had to pick a spot, it would be down in the Mississippi Delta. The birth of the blues coincides with the emancipation of the slaves and their transition from slavery to sharecropping. This change was only a slightly better deal for these African Americans, who essentially became indentured servants.

Blues music itself has roots in African rhythms, spirituals, and church music, with the African style call and response. New Orleans jazz man Sidney Bechet called the blues the secular side of black music. He said, "The blues, like spirituals, were prayers. One was praying to God and the other was praying to man. They were both the same thing in a way; they were both my people's way of praying to be themselves, praying to be let alone so they could be human."

In the post-emancipation era, which is roughly between 1870 and 1900, juke joints opened up all over the South. These were ramshackle places where blacks went after a backbreaking day's work to listen to music, dance, and drink.

Because blues was the first nonwhite music to take hold in the larger popular culture, it predates rock 'n' roll and rap as being the "devil's music." White folks considered it disreputable and said that it incited violence, maybe even provoked much dreaded sexual behavior.

W. C. Handy, a deeply religious man from Alabama who always looked dapper in suit, tie, and pocket square, has been called the "Father of the Blues" even though he came along a good 20 to 30 years after the birth of the blues. He was, however, the first to make the music popular with nonblack audiences, even playing at Carnegie Hall in 1928.

The New Orleans style of blues is a variation that developed in the 1940s and '50s in and around the city. Rooted in the blues music going back a generation, the New Orleans style is strongly influenced by the strut of Dixieland jazz and the Caribbean sounds so prevalent in the area. The music is dominated here by piano and horn rather than the Robert Johnson guitar style heard everywhere else. New Orleans blues has the cheerful and lazy feel of good-time music, no matter how somber the lyrics may be. Some worthy blues musicians will be absent. Y'all ought to go to the library (if you still do such a retro thing) or Google the blues artists like Babe Stovall. He said often before performing, "I ain't the best in the world, but I'll do until the best git here." He's actually good enough to deserve your attention.

Guitar Slim and Slim Harpo

The earliest stars of New Orleans blues were Slim and Slim. Guitar Slim, lesser known as Eddie Jones, is best known for his classic, million-copy-selling song, "The Things That I Used to Do." It's listed on the Rock and Roll Hall of Fame's "500 Songs That Shaped Rock 'n' Roll." With his experiments and distorted overtones on the electric guitar, Guitar Slim also greatly influenced many future guitarists, including Jimi Hendrix.

Slim Harpo, a.k.a. James Moore, was a leading exponent of the swamp blues style and one of the most commercially successful blues artists of his day. His hit songs include "I'm a King Bee" and "Rainin' In My Heart," as well as "Baby Scratch My Back," which reached #1 on the R&B chart and #16 on the US pop chart. A master of the blues harmonica, his stage name was derived from the popular nickname for that instrument, the "harp."

Never able to be a full-time musician, Harpo had his own trucking business to make ends meet when he wasn't on tour and playing in the studio for other musicians. His harmonica can be heard on albums by The Rolling Stones, the Yardbirds, The Kinks, and Pink Floyd. The Moody Blues took their name from an instrumental track of Slim's called "Moody Blues." Set to gain wider fame on a European tour, Slim Harpo died of a heart attack at age 46.

Champion Jack Dupree

Champion Jack Dupree was orphaned at the age of 2 and sent to the New Orleans Colored Waifs Home, the same place as Louis Armstrong. He went on to become a "spy boy" for the Yellow Pocahontas "tribe" of Mardi Gras Indians (revelers) and, encouraged by heavyweight champion Joe Louis, a boxer who won 107 bouts and a Golden Gloves championship, giving him his lifelong nickname.

Dupree's piano playing was all straight blues and boogie-woogie. He was not a sophisticated musician or singer; he sang about his life, mostly jail, drinking, and drug addiction. His song "Big Leg Emma's" is said to be the roots of rap music. Some

Champion Jack Dupree and Mickey Baker   Creative Commons/Sescenti

of his saucier lyrics include lines like, "Mama, move your false teeth, papa wanna scratch your gums."

His biggest commercial success was "Walkin' the Blues," which led to several national tours, and eventually to a European tour.

In later years Champion Jack recorded with John Mayall, Eric Clapton, and The Band. Jerry Lee Lewis "borrowed" heavily from Dupree's "Shake Baby Shake" for his signature hit "Whole Lotta Shakin' Goin' On."

Snooks Eaglin

Also called Blind Snooks Eaglin, Snooks Eaglin had a vocal style compared to Ray Charles. Like Ray Charles he lost his eyesight as a very young man; Snooks was 2, Ray Charles was 7. Eaglin was completely self-taught as a musician by listening to and playing along with the radio. In his late teens, he would sometimes bill himself as "Little Ray Charles." His range was legendary. Eaglin could play blues, rock and roll, jazz, country, and Latin. He claimed in interviews that his musical repertoire included some 2,500 songs, earning him the nickname, The Human Jukebox.

As a 16-year-old, he joined the Flamingoes, a local seven-piece band started by Allen Toussaint. The Flamingoes did not have a bass player, and according to Eaglin, he played both the guitar and the bass parts at the same time. When the Flamingoes dissolved in the '50s, Eaglin set off on a solo career, teaming up with various top musicians like George Porter Jr., James "Sugar Boy" Crawford, Smokey Johnson, and the great James Booker. At live shows, he did not usually prepare set lists. Instead, he played songs that came to his head or by request from the audience, which often drove his bandmates crazy.

One of my regrets in life is that time and again I meant to go hear Snooks Eaglin at the Mid-City Rock 'n' Bowl while visiting New Orleans, before I moved here. But I always got distracted, as New Orleans can distract you. I figured I could catch him "next time," because he played there regularly. The bowling alley/dance hall used to sell a T-shirt stamped: "There ain't nothing more New Orleans than Snooks Eaglin playing at the Mid-City Rock 'n' Bowl." By the time we actually moved to New Orleans, Snooks had passed away.

CHAPTER 4

Go Ramblin'
(Where to Hear Live Blues Tonight)

There's a difference between the blues of the New Orleans guys and anyone else and the difference is in a chord, but I can't figure the name of it. It's a different chord, and they all make it.

—Jimmy Rushing

There are nowhere near as many blues musicians playing in New Orleans tonight as there are jazz performers. But, many of those who do play carry that "Must Do" tag.

Little Freddie King

Little Freddie King is playing somewhere this week, quite possibly tonight. He's a regular at BJ's Lounge, d.b.a., and Old Arabi Bar, occasionally playing at Le Bon Temps Roule or Ruby's Roadhouse. And if there's a blues festival anywhere, he's no doubt part of the lineup. He's played the Jazz & Heritage Festival 42 times and counting.

You'd be a fool not to go to one of his gigs. His blues is raw and it's real. King has been tabbed "one of the last great country-blues players." He is undeniably the King of New Orleans current blues scene. Local music writer Robert Fontenot perfectly captured his music: "It ain't pretty . . . you can practically smell the Chinese food and chicken coming from Chun King . . . the slop bucket wheeze put out on his cover of King Curtis's 'Soul Twist' is potent enough to turn George W. Bush into the Godfather of Soul. It's *that* country and *that* ghetto."

King was born Fread E. Martin in McComb, Mississippi, just under two hours outside New Orleans. As a child, he crafted a makeshift guitar from an old cigar box and six long hairs plucked from a horse's tail, and begged his father to teach him to play. A school bus trip brought him to New Orleans for the first time. He remembers, "When I get down here, everything was popping and everybody was jumping

and everybody was having good times. And I said, 'Wow, this is the place where I'm supposed to be at.'

Shortly thereafter, he jumped a train and moved to New Orleans. He was 14 years old. He began to land gigs, but not in the swankiest of clubs. The Busy Bee on Perdido Street he later immortalized in his song "Bucket of Blood," so named because of the frequency of patrons being shot or stabbed there. He worked his way into the legendary Dew Drop Inn, where he played backup to the female impersonator Patsy Vidalia. King has survived rough rooms, alcoholism, and a wife who shot him five times. He immortalized her in his song "Mean Little Woman."

Tonight (or tomorrow night) the now-75-year-old blues master will be in a club, dressed in a sharp suit, alligator shoes, and skull-emblazoned guitar strap slung over his shoulder.

Walter "Wolfman" Washington

Though Walter "Wolfman" Washington does blend in funk and R&B to create his own unique sound, he has his roots deeply imbedded in blues music. I place him in this chapter for convenience, but Washington has received awards not just as Best Blues Performer, but also Best R&B/Funk Artist and Best Guitarist. He's a masterful guitar player with a great, nickname-producing howl of a voice. Wolfman has been performing since the '60s, first invited to join Lee Dorsey's band, then forming his own All Fools Band. In the 1970s, he joined Johnny Adams's band and played with Adams for 20 years. During this time he continued to work as a solo artist, and in the late '70s formed another band of his own, the Roadmasters, which is still going strong.

It wasn't until 20 years on stage that Washington released his first solo album, *Rainin' In My Life*.

Washington plays around town each week, most frequently every Wednesday at the music club d.b.a, and often at Maple Leaf Bar.

Andy J. Forest

Early in his career Andy Forest was a wild man of a performer, going way past whatever Little Richard or Jerry Lee Lewis might do on stage. His theme song was "I Got Crazy Legs," during which he did his crazy leg dance. The rest of the set would be a frenzy of stomping, shouting, and whooping it up on the harmonica. Invariably he would include his signature move, playing the harmonica while standing on his head. "I wanted to do something that would excite the audience," he said.

But it reached the point where people would come to his shows and say, "Hey, are you gonna stand on your head and play harmonica tonight?" He realized his theatrics were overshadowing his music.

In more recent years, his music has evolved to be a low-key, back-porch blues style. During his weekly shows every Tuesday and Friday at The Spotted Cat he accompanies himself on harmonica, Dobro, and a guitar made from boards that were taken from his house. He sings in a smoky baritone that is perfectly suited to the poetic detailed stories about his life in New Orleans. He writes songs about his daughter, "Ella Dora," his home in Bywater, and driving to and from work. He also wrote "Let 'Em Die," a Katrina protest song about how the government sent body bags to the city but failed to send food and water.

Forest can be seen additional times each week as a member of the Washboard Chaz Blues Trio.

Washboard Chaz

Originally from New York, Washboard Chaz lived in Boulder some 22 years, and didn't show up in New Orleans until 2000. He has since become an integral part of our music scene and is counted among the best acoustic blues performers in New Orleans.

He's as much promiscuous as he is prodigious, playing with The Iguanas, New Orleans Jazz Vipers, The Palmetto Bug Stompers, New Orleans Nightcrawlers, Tuba Fats, Royal Fingerbowl, Washboard Rodeo, and his two main bands, the Tin Men and the Washboard Chaz Blues Trio.

He's just as indiscriminate with his settings. In a one-week stretch, Chaz can be heard at d.b.a., The Spotted Cat, Blue Nile, Three Muses, 21st Amendment, and The Columns Hotel.

He's accomplished all this as a musician whose only instrument is his tricked-out washboard and finger thimbles.

One of his lasting claims to fame is ChazFest, held each year at the same time as Jazz & Heritage Festival. What happened was that every musician in town wanted to play at the 2006 Jazz Fest, the first after Hurricane Katrina, as a way to give back to the city. Washboard Chaz, among many, did not make the cut to appear. Rather than sulking or seething, he had the idea to do his own music festival. Tin Men bandmate Alex McMurray has an enormous common garden in the back of his house. This became the site of this alternative fest with a lineup of alternative musicians.

Jazz & Heritage Festival will draw in Bruce Springsteen, Lenny Kravitz, and local luminaries. But it also draws a half-million attendees, meaning you often watch live performers digitally presented on a huge stadium screen while standing behind a few tens of thousands of fans. ChazFest is a more intimate setting for seeing musicians like New Dopey Singers, War Amps, Mas Mamones, Sarah Quintana, and Rory Danger and the Danger Dangers, bands you may not know . . . yet.

Tab Benoit

Benoit's playing combines a number of blues styles, primarily Delta blues. He's won the B. B. King Entertainer of the Year award, the Best Contemporary Male Performer at the Blues Music Awards (formerly the W. C. Handy Awards), and received a Grammy nomination for Best Traditional Blues Album.

He is also a tireless advocate for conservation. Benoit is the founder and spokesman for Voice of the Wetlands, an organization working to save Louisiana's coastal wetlands. The Governor's Award for Conservationist of the Year joins his music awards.

When not on tour, Tab Benoit can be heard regularly at Rock 'n' Bowl.

John Mooney

The first time I heard John Mooney on the radio, I thought I was listening to John Hiatt. The slide guitar, the voice—there is a strong similarity. But after learning I was really hearing a New Orleans–based artist, I dug around YouTube and spent some time at the listening stations at Louisiana Music Factory. I realized this was something even better: a John Hiatt sound enhanced by combining Delta blues and New Orleans funk.

Mooney is actually from East Orange, New Jersey. He left home when he was 15 and within the year had the good fortune to meet Mississippi blues legend Son House. Impressed by the young man's talent, Son and John became friends. Mooney has said, "I wasn't aware of what the opportunity meant, but I knew there was nobody better in Delta blues."

Mooney moved to New Orleans in 1976 and began playing with a host of A-level musicians that included Earl King, The Meters, Snooks Eaglin, and Professor Longhair. He released his first album *Comin' Your Way* on Blind Pig Records in 1979. Two years later he formed his own band, Bluesiana. He has been recording and touring with them ever since.

His work has been heralded as "a seductive musical cocktail that leaves you deliriously drunk with pleasure every time" (*Blues Access* magazine) and "bumps, grinds, and simmers with the emotional intensity of a musician who plays directly from his soul to yours" (*Blues Revue* magazine).

While he doesn't do regular gigs, John Mooney can be heard now and again at Little Gem Saloon, Carrollton Station, and Tipitina's. He also appears most every year at Jazz & Heritage Festival.

SPOTLIGHT

Frenchmen Street

The most concentrated and best place to hear live blues (and jazz, and funk, and brass band, and maybe a little reggae) is Frenchmen Street in the Marigny neighborhood. It has replaced Bourbon Street as the live music street of New Orleans. It's our version of Beale Street in Memphis or 6th Street in Austin (only much, much better). Twelve clubs are packed door-to-door in two-and-a-half blocks. The performers are drastically better than the current Bourbon Street cover bands that butcher '70s hits by Journey and Foreigner, and there are no 18-year-old boys threatening to throw up on you. I might be tempted to suggest you go see Meschiya Lake at The Spotted Cat, or John Boutté at d.b.a., or the venerable Ellis Marsalis at Snug Harbor. But in truth the best way to "do" Frenchmen is not to have a specific club. Instead, just go and let your ears be your guide. There's always a brass band playing on the street, and there is also a nightly outdoor art market, strung with decorative lights, where local artisans sell jewelry, photography, fashion, and paintings.

Apple Barrel

609 Frenchmen St.
Phone: 504-949-9399

A tiny bar below the restaurant hosts nightly music in a funky setting. The place is decorated with dollar bills taped to the walls behind the bar, and a mural of Louis Armstrong hangs where the musicians play. Originally it was the setting where the late Coco Robicheaux replaced the jukebox and dartboard as the entertainment.

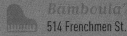

Bamboula's

514 Frenchmen St.

Phone: 504-944-8461

Opened in 2013, Bamboula's is the newest kid on the block. This is a regular stop for Smoky Greenwell, the Messy Cookers, John Lisi, Troy Turner, and their own Bamboula's Hot Trio.

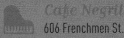

Blue Nile

532 Frenchmen St.

Phone: 504-948-2583

Blue Nile is the most eclectic, or at least the most wide-ranging, of the clubs that line Frenchmen. On its two stages you can hear most any kind of music from New Orleans's top-line jazz performers like Kermit Ruffins. You can also expect plenty of brass band, hip hop, and an occasional taste of indie rock music. The club also hosts weekly reggae dance parties with DJ T-Roy.

Cafe Negril

606 Frenchmen St.

Phone: 504-944-4744

Their Mexican food, which I've never tried, garners a range of comments online, from "Best Tacos" to "Burrito Bust." The music is more consistently thumbs up. John Lisi & Delta Funk, a blues band with a little funk, plays on Tuesdays and Saturdays. Dana Abbott, singer, songwriter, and HBO *Treme* star, performs Fridays and Sundays. The Higher Heights Reggae Band seems the most suited for this stage, which has a huge Bob Marley mural covering the wall. Unlike most clubs on Frenchmen, Cafe Negril has a sizable dance floor.

d.b.a.

616 Frenchmen St.

Phone: 504-942-3731

As one of the gems of Frenchmen Street, d.b.a. is an attractive club with high ceilings, paneled walls, and a lineup of New Orleans's finest musicians performing two times each night at 6:00 or 7:00, and a second show at 10:00. The music offerings span a full range, from jazz (Glen David Andrews), jazz vocalist (John Boutté), blues (Walter "Wolfman" Washington), brass band (Treme Brass Band), funk and R&B (Jon Cleary), Mardi Gras Indians (Big Chief Monk Boudreaux), swamp pop (Palmetto Bug Stompers), and even flamenco (Ven Pa' Ca).

Dragon's Den

435 Esplanade Ave.

Phone: 504-940-5546

The bright red Dragon's Den is technically not on Frenchmen Street. It's just around the corner, and so fits with a nighttime of Frenchmen club hopping. The front room is the setting for live bands like

the Bayou Saints, Up Up We Go (a jazz ensemble), and Loose Marbles. The venue is also used for DJ-themed nights. The upstairs room hosts the burlesque show "Talk Nerdy to Me" on Saturday nights and features electronic dance parties on others.

Maison
508 Frenchmen St.
Phone: 504-371-5543

Maison is the largest venue on Frenchmen. The three-story building has a front-room stage, a back room used for big shows (most weekends), and an upstairs room with a balcony that is used for private parties. They also serve better-than-passable Creole food.

Snug Harbor Jazz Bistro
626 Frenchmen St.
Phone: 504-949-0696

You eat in one room and then slide over to the music room where each night's performer plays two sets, one at 8:00 and a second at 10:00. Charmaine Neville on Monday nights has been their mainstay for years. She is a part of the famous Neville clan, daughter of saxophonist Charles Neville. Charmaine overcame CADASIL (Cerebral Autosomal-Dominant Arteriopathy with Subcortical Infarcts and Leukoencephalopathy) in 2012, and she continues to deliver her popular jazz funk singing with noteworthy dance moves. The Marsalis clan practically fills up the rest of the week with Delfeayo playing on Wednesdays, father Ellis on Fridays, and Wynton and Jason making guest appearances. More recently, the Stanton Moore Trio has become the draw Tuesday nights.

30° × 90°

520 Frenchmen St.

30° × 90° is the latitude and longitude of New Orleans, the name of an all-female blues band, and also this cozy club with cocktails, decent pizza, and live music.

The Spotted Cat Music Club

623 Frenchmen St.
Phone: 504-943-3887

Their website says they're known by locals as "The CAT." I've only lived in New Orleans for six years (and have been visiting at least once a year for 32 years), and I've never heard them called that even once. They are, however, assuming the mantle as one of New Orleans's top music spots. With no cover charge (they do require a one drink minimum) and among the best musicians each night (most often three performers each night), if you don't come early, it's very likely you'll stand, or rather sway and shimmy, the entire night in a lively elbow-to-ass-cheek crowd.

"The Spot," as now called by me alone, starts live performances earlier than the other Frenchmen clubs, sometimes as early as 2:00 p.m. Regulars Andy J. Forest (Tuesdays and Fridays) and Sarah McCoy (Mondays and Thursdays) go on at 4:00 p.m. Washboard Chaz (Fridays), Meschiya Lake (Tuesdays), and the Panorama Jazz Band (Saturdays) are the 6:00 p.m. slot. The late sets (10:00 p.m.) are occupied by jazz troupes, the New Orleans Jazz Vipers (Mondays), the Cottonmouth Kings (Fridays), and Smoking Time Jazz Club (Tuesdays).

There's no reservations, no food in the bar, and, as proclaimed by the hand-painted sign by a locally renowned artist, Simon, there's to be "No Drinks or Drunks on the Pianee."

Three Muses
536 Frenchmen St.
Phone: 504-252-4801

The three muses intended here are food, spirits (the alcoholic kind), and music. The featured musicians include Luke Winslow King, a unique slide guitarist who mixes Delta blues with ragtime and small sips of rock 'n' roll. Glen David Andrews is recognized as among our best trombone players, along with Trombone Shorty. The Shotgun Jazz Band recalls the hot, bluesy, no-frills jazz melodies that yesteryear poured from New Orleans's dance halls. And the Hot Club of New Orleans has an almost missionary zeal to champion the swing-era music of Duke Ellington, Django Reinhardt, and Stephane Grappelli, though they infuse this classic sound with their own modern sensibilities.

Vaso
500 Frenchmen St.
Phone: 504-272-0929

The lounge-lizard setting hosts brass bands, DJs, and decent food.

Yuki Izakaya
525 Frenchmen St.
Phone: 504-943-1122

This new-ish Japanese tavern serves homestyle tapas and many small plates with a wide selection of sake and shochu, as well as Japanese beers. Yuki doubles as a dimly lit late night haunt with live music each night. The performers tend toward the peculiar like the cabaret-style goth band, Morella & the Wheels of If.

CHAPTER 5

R&B and Funk

I don't leave home without Professor Longhair in my head or somewhere in my anatomy.

—Allen Toussaint

Here the lines get a little messy. The musicians I profiled in the jazz and blues chapters have, on occasion, dipped a toe into R&B, funk, and other styles. It's a jazz thing to adapt and improvise and merge other styles. It's a New Orleans thing to always jambalaya it up. We are a mixed-race Creole city. Our cuisine, mostly French, borrows heavily from West Africa, Spain, and Native American cultures. And then toss in a little German and Irish and the dish is complete. Our musical flavors include Caribbean, gospel, blues, you name it.

The artists I include in this chapter are here mostly on the basis of whim, feelings, and my unjustifiable opinions. Walter "Wolfman" Washington was mentioned in association with the blues chapter, but he could have been noted here. The great Professor Longhair could go anywhere in this book, just pick a chapter. I chose to note him here.

Rhythm and blues was originally coined by record companies to describe recordings marketed predominantly to urban African Americans. It replaced the term "race music," after it was deemed offensive. Go figure. R&B song lyrics usually focus on the ups and downs in relationships, finances, and well . . . sex. New Orleans R&B is characterized by extensive use of piano and horn sections, and our complex syncopated "second line" rhythms.

The term "funk" goes all the way back to the beginning of jazz and Buddy Bolden's signature song, "Funky Butt." This music is rhythmically based on a two-celled onbeat/offbeat structure, which originated in sub-Saharan African music traditions. The New Orleans style appropriated the bifurcated structure from the Afro-Cuban mambo and conga. Now, in plain English, that simply means that funk music is slow, loose, "sexy," riff-oriented, and danceable (or at least sway-able).

I probably should open the following artist descriptions with Fats Domino, but I'm going to save him for the chapter on New Orleans history of unbelievable piano masters. Instead, I'll start with the lesser-known heroes of R&B and funk.

Lloyd Price

Lloyd Price is widely called Mr. Personality, a nickname taken from one of his better-known hits, "Personality," released in 1959. His biggest R&B hit, "Lawdy Miss Clawdy," was an original song produced by Dave Bartholomew and featured (though we're not talking about him yet) Fats Domino on piano. "Lawdy Miss Clawdy" topped the R&B charts for seven weeks. It was thereafter widely covered by decades of musicians, such as Elvis Presley, The Buckinghams, John Lennon, and Elvis Costello.

After serving in the military, Price returned to New Orleans and launched KRC (Kent Record Company) with Harold Logan, a longtime friend and collaborator. Here he recorded "Stagger Lee,"—no, maybe *that* was his biggest hit—which also topped the pop and R&B charts.

Price has all but left the music business, and he currently manages Icon Food Brands. They make a line of Southern-style food, including Lawdy Miss Clawdy food products, ranging from canned greens to sweet potato cookies. They also make Lloyd Price's Soulful 'n' Smooth Grits and Lloyd Price's Energy-2-Eat Bar (branded "Good taste . . . Great Personality").

Shirley & Lee

Shirley Goodman and Leonard Lee were branded Sweethearts of the Blues, even though they weren't sweethearts and their music wasn't the blues. However, their #1 biggest hit is not in doubt. They recorded "Let the Good Times Roll" in 1956. The song has been covered by Sonny & Cher, Bunny Sigler, The Righteous Brothers, Delbert McClinton, Barbra Streisand, The Searchers, Whiskey Howl, Joe Strummer of The Clash, Harry Nilsson, Roy Orbison, The Youngbloods, Conway Twitty, Slade, Freddy Fender, Buckwheat Zydeco, The Animals, Fishbone, The Kingsmen, and The Sonics. The funkiest rendition is by George Clinton, featuring the Red Hot Chili Peppers and Kim Manning.

Their other massive hits were "Feel So Good" and "I'm Gone," which was covered by The Rolling Stones, Barbra Streisand, The Righteous Brothers, and Roy Orbison. Their songs created a fictionalized soap opera story of Shirley & Lee's made-up relationship. Fans would buy the singles simply to keep up with the continuing saga of the two (not really) sweethearts. Their heartbreaker song "Shirley Come Back to Me" was followed up by "Shirley's Back."

Shirley & Lee almost never sang in harmony, and not very often together at all. Their contrasting male-female duet style was influential on early ska and reggae styles.

The Dixie Cups

Sisters Barbara and Rosa Hawkins and their cousin Joan Johnson had been casually singing together since grade school. When a local talent competition had a cancellation, the girls were asked to step in just to fill the time slot. This led to them being "discovered." They were whisked to New York where they recorded a few songs, and they came back to New Orleans with no real expectations. Rosa Hawkins remembers the next step as told to NPR, "The first time I heard 'Chapel of Love' on the radio, it was on a Saturday morning and I was doing my chores. This record came on and it was like, 'Oh, that record sounds familiar. Oh, I know that song.' And then I realized, 'Hey! That's my voice there!'"

"Chapel of Love" would knock The Beatles out of the #1 spot, and it would stay #1 for three weeks. The reverse side of the 45 came about when the three girls were fooling around in the recording studio while everyone else was taking a break. They started singing an old Mardi Gras Indian chant, and the New York control-room guys were blown away, having never heard anything like it. That song, "Iko Iko," would become a Top 20 hit and a New Orleans standard.

The name Dixie Cups was foisted on them, thank God, just before their first record release. They had been called Little Miss and the Muffets. They rarely perform now, but did reunite for the 2015 Jazz Fest.

Dave Bartholomew

Chances are this is the first you've heard of Dave Bartholomew, but he ranks among the most important individuals in the history of New Orleans music. His greatest accomplishments were executed behind the scenes. He was a songwriter, talent scout, arranger, and general man-about-town. His greatest successes came through his partnership with Fats Domino. The two collaborated on 40 hit songs.

Bartholomew did record some of his own material. His song "My Ding-a-Ling" became a huge hit, and was a cover later recorded by Chuck Berry. This song was in fact Chuck Berry's only #1 hit in his long career. Many radio stations refused to play either Bartholomew's or Berry's version of "My Ding-a-Ling" because of the double entendre of ding-a-ling. By today's standards this song is as tame as a Ritz cracker.

Will Howcraft

Professor Longhair

The funkiest of the funk, without a doubt, is Professor Longhair. Born Henry Roeland "Roy" Byrd, he began playing music as a boy on the streets of New Orleans after he discovered an abandoned upright piano in an alley. Some believe his idiosyncratic and completely original style was the result of learning to play on a busted piano missing some keys and strings.

There's a current phrase printed on T-shirts and bumper stickers from Dirty Coast Press that states, "Listen to Your City." This was never more true than Professor Longhair. He taught himself to play by soaking up influences from everything he heard on the streets of New Orleans and outside the clubs he was too young to enter. Barrelhouse boogie-woogie, Caribbean rhythms like the rumba (many of his relatives were West Indian), and second line parade rhythms were all in the mix.

Unlike the many preteen jazz musicians, Professor Longhair (also known as Fess) was 30 years old when he began to work professionally as a musician. Until then, he'd gotten by as a prizefighter, a gambler, and a vaudeville dancer.

In 1949, he formed his group, Professor Longhair and His Shuffling Hungarians. The group was given the name by Mike Tessitore, owner of Caldonia Club, for all the band members who had long hair, which was uncharacteristic at the time. The following year, Fess was signed by Mercury Records and his "Baldhead" reached #5 on Billboard's R&B chart. Longhair later recorded on more than a dozen labels but never caught on as a star because of a combination of poor health, mismanagement, and probably the primary reason why Professor Longhair never took off commercially had to do with his unique style. Tony Russell, in his classic book *The Blues*, writes: "The vivacious rhumba-rhythmed piano blues and choked singing typical of Fess were too weird to sell millions of records."

Professor Longhair abandoned music altogether in 1964 to work odd jobs. Allen Toussaint was shocked one day when he visited a record store on Rampart Street and discovered that his musical hero was working the back room as a stock clerk. After languishing in total obscurity, Professor Longhair was rediscovered by talent scouts for the New Orleans Jazz & Heritage Festival. They asked him to play at the second-ever festival in 1971. He performed at every New Orleans Festival thereafter until his death in 1980.

Professor Longhair is now hailed as "the Picasso of keyboard funk" and "the Bach of rock." His style profoundly influenced many of New Orleans's best known musicians, including Mac Rebennack (a.k.a. Dr. John), Fats Domino, Huey "Piano" Smith, James Booker, The Meters, the Neville Brothers, and Allen Toussaint. Many of his songs like "Tipitina" and "Big Chief" have become essential lexicons of New Orleans music. "Tipitina," the song, is supposedly about a French Quarter woman with no toes who was, quite literally, Tippy Tina. His "Mardi Gras in New Orleans" serves as the soundtrack to Carnival season every year.

The Meters

The popularity of funk music can be attributed to one man, and he is the non-New Orleanian James Brown, the Godfather of Soul. James Brown, however, schooled off The Meters. The Meters never broke into the mainstream, but they were an extraordinary live band, packing houses in New Orleans and having a below-the-radar reputation as being the hottest thing going.

The four original members were Art Neville on keyboards, George Porter Jr. on bass, Leo Nocentelli on guitar, and Zigaboo Modeliste on drums. Cyril Neville joined The Meters as a vocalist and percussionist in the 1970s. They performed and recorded their own unique music from the late 1960s until 1977. The band played

SPOTLIGHT

 Tipitina's
501 Napoleon Ave.
Phone: 504-895-8477

The iconic club was created in 1977 by young music fans, The Fabulous Fo'teen, who wanted to ensure that Professor Longhair always had a place to play his weird rumba-boogie. Not only was his style too out there at the time to be appreciated everywhere but Fess also had burned too many bridges in the French Quarter.

The club is named for one of Longhair's most enigmatic recordings, "Tipitina." The club has a large single room that can easily accommodate more than 1,000 people. As you enter the front door, you'll meet a bust of Professor Longhair right in front of you. I guess you could rub it for good mojo, just as you might rub the nose of Lincoln's bronze statue in Springfield, Illinois or rub the bronze fannies of the Riviera Hotel's Crazy Girls to increase your gambler's odds in Vegas. I've never seen anyone do it. I've never done it. You can be the first.

Tipitina's is one of the premier, no make that the #1 hotbed, destinations of New Orleans's live music scene. The venue helped launch the careers of the Neville Brothers, Harry Connick Jr., Dr. John, and many others. An all-star cast has played and continues to play Tipitina's. The acts include The Meters, Cowboy Mouth, the Radiators, Galactic, Better Than Ezra, and Trombone Shorty. National artists playing there include, or have included Wilco, Nine Inch Nails, Pearl Jam, Lenny Kravitz, Bonnie Raitt, James Brown, Widespread Panic, Stevie Ray Vaughan, Tim McGraw, Goo Goo Dolls, Parliament Funkadelic, Robert Cray, Patti Smith, Willie Nelson, Buddy Guy, Dresden Dolls, and Medeski, Martin & Wood.

When my friends Jenny and Brian visited from the DC area, I took them to a three-set night at Tipitina's. I watched them as they slowly melted into the music, at first loving Sweet Crude, then loving Helen Gillet even more . . . and by the time The Wild Magnolias hit the stage, I knew New Orleans and our music had seduced them for life.

Jason S / Creative Commons

a hugely influential role as the backing musicians for other artists, including Lee Dorsey, Robert Palmer, and Dr. John. They developed a fanatical following, among them Paul McCartney and Mick Jagger. Rickey Vincent, in his book *Funk*, wrote, "In and outside of New Orleans, people came to understand that they were the core of a revolution in rhythm."

After eight acclaimed albums, The Meters became frustrated by their lack of commercial success. It all fell apart for them in 1977.

Their songs "Cissy Strut" and "Look-Ka Py Py" are considered funk classics today. Their sound is unquestionably the basis for much of the hip hop of the '80s and '90s. Hip hop artist Zach "DJ Z-Trip" Sciacca says that The Meters' catalog of songs remains required material for any aspiring turntablist. "They're like DJing 101."

The Batiste Clan

Where the Marsalis clan is the first family of jazz, the Batiste family could be said to be their equal in funk (plus R&B, blues, and yes, jazz, too). They are the largest musical family in the South, and at one time there could be as many as 23 Batistes on a single stage.

Perhaps the best known at the moment is Jon Batiste. The under-30-year-old has already performed in more than 40 countries, in Carnegie Hall, at Lincoln Center, and at the Kennedy Center. His high-profile collaborators include Lenny Kravitz, Jimmy Buffett, Harry Connick Jr., and Wynton Marsalis. He has appeared on magazine covers as the leader for Stephen Colbert's new Late Show Band. But perhaps his greatest accomplishment is making the harmonaboard look cool.

He has said that within his family "music spreads like a disease." Estella and Jean Batiste, the matriarch and patriarch of the clan, met in New York City and settled in New Orleans. They had seven boys, inspired them toward music, and assembled the Batiste Brothers Band. At least one Batiste has played with most every major New Orleans musical group, from Professor Longhair's group, to the Olympia Brass and Treme Brass Bands and the Dirty Dozen Brass Band, to The Funky Meters, which is a reincarnation of the original band, The Meters.

The brood includes Harold Battiste, a record label founder, composer, and saxophonist, who predates Jon as a TV show bandleader (Harold was the band director for the Sonny and Cher Show). Percussionist Damon Batiste has performed with other prominent bands, recording with the Dirty Dozen Brass Band and George Clinton and the P-Funk All-Stars. Damon also played a vital role in the development of Frenchmen Street as New Orleans's music hub. Trumpeter and educator Milton Batiste used to lead the Olympia Brass Band. David Russell Batiste has been playing the drums since he was 4. He still plays regularly around the city in a trio with Joe Krown and Walter "Wolfman" Washington. The late and beloved Treme Brass Band leader Lionel Batiste was more than a musician. He was an ambassador for the city, often seen around town dressed (for no particular reason) in his finest suits, bowler hat, two-tone shoes, and his signature watch, draped across his fingers rather than on his wrist, because he "always wanted to have time on my hands." Kermit Ruffins said of Uncle Lionel: "He taught me how to act, how to dress, how to feel about life."

"With the Batiste family," Russell Batiste has said, "we are all dependent on one another to survive—musically, mentally, in life. I learned everything from my dad's six brothers. As a kid out in the streets, I was playing under them, trying to soak up their lifestyles, their music. If you can't depend on your family, you're just a lost soul on this earth."

King James & the Special Men

I don't know whether to classify King James & the Special Men as R&B or blues or rock, but since Alex Rawls wrote that they are "the champions of New Orleans classic R&B," let's go with that. The band calls themselves R&B&D, rhythm and blues and drunk. They used to be called one of New Orleans's best kept secrets. However, the cats were let out of the bag when *The New York Times* wrote, "One of New Orleans's premier bands, King James & The Special Men . . . As the first few bars of sweaty rhythm and blues hit the room, what had at first seemed like a random collection of disconnected souls became a unified and joyful mass. Many began to dance, on their own with palpable abandon and in pairs, the boys swinging the girls around the makeshift dance floor, as if we'd all teleported to some out-of-the-way roadhouse from the '50s."

After five years playing every Monday night at BJ's Lounge, in the summer of 2015 they moved walking distance to Sidney's Saloon (1200 St. Bernard Ave.). Every Monday night, frontman Jimmy Horn still brings the red beans and rice.

Flow Tribe

Founded in 2004 by six high school friends, Flow Tribe represents one of the hotter next-generation New Orleans bands. They have grown to become what they call, "A relentlessly touring band that plays major venues and festivals around the country bringing with them a heat and passion." They headline national venues like SXSW in Austin and our Voodoo Music + Arts Experience, French Quarter Festival, and Jazz & Heritage Festival the last five years running. For some reason known only to the band and the Steel City, they love Pittsburgh and play there often. Locally, they play (rarely) in small clubs like The Maison, but they perform at most festivals. The band was also featured heavily on MTV's *Real World: New Orleans*.

Flow Tribe plays a classic style of funk, their horns and pop sensibility recounting early-'90s ska. Their guitar work, featuring the Cuban-born Mario Palmisano, displays a Caribbean and reggae influence. Their polyrhythmic percussion is pure New Orleans. Like the Beastie Boys, their music makes you want to dance and rage at the same time.

Says Flow Tribe's washboard and harmonica player, John-Michael Early: "You won't hear us do a lot of ballads. We're not going to cry with you. But if you are crying, we'll help you forget whatever's troubling you."

The Neville Brothers

Hardly the "other" family of funk, the Neville Brothers are probably more famous than the Bastiste clan. Brothers Art, Charles, Aaron, and Cyril don't *act* gangsta like some rap artist wannabes because they *were* gangsta. They grew up in poverty in the city's Calliope housing project, and when Aaron was 17 he went to jail for six months for stealing a car. He later was caught robbing a fur store and spent a year in jail. Plus, he was a longtime heroin addict. Charles spent three years in the Louisiana state pen for possession of marijuana. He also was busted several times for shoplifting, the most brazen being when he put on a khaki shirt with GEORGE embroidered over the pocket, slid a pencil behind his ear, grabbed a clipboard, and walked into a store on Canal Street. He then strapped a refrigerator onto a hand truck and walked right out with it.

It was their uncle, George Landy, also known as Big Chief Jolly of the Wild Tchoupitoulas, who reeled in and redirected the boys. After their mother died, Big Chief Jolly got them to forget any mischief they were into and all take part in his 1976 recording session. They had performed together earlier as the Hawketts and had a local hit with the song "Mardi Gras Mambo." In between jail stints, Aaron Neville sang the classic, "Tell It like It Is." He was, and is, famous for an angelic voice that comes out of a bricklayer's body. When he was 8 or 9, Aaron would sing his way into movies or basketball games. Whoever was working on the door, he recalled, knew he could sing, so they'd say, "All right, Neville, sing me a song and I'll let you in."

Something special happened when the brothers made music together again for their uncle. They decided to create the Neville Brothers band. The newly opened Tipitina's invited them to perform, and word spread quickly about this new pop, funk, and soul band of brothers. Within weeks the Neville Brothers at Tipitina's became a hit. They played to a packed house of people jiving to the music and doing the Gator. (Gatoring is basically dry humping to a drumbeat.) These early high-energy sessions at Tipitina's became the stuff of legend. Far more people claimed to have made that scene than ever could have fit inside the club.

The Neville Brothers became fiercely popular in the area and overseas. "In Europe, they always went insane over our stuff," said Aaron. "But here in America, no one would book us, except in Louisiana and Texas. We had a gold record in France and were practically unknown here."

Their one sister, Athelgra, also had a brief singing career with the Dixie Cups. Aaron's son Ivan on keys and Art's son Ian on guitar started Dumpstaphunk in 2003 as an intended one-night-only performance. They went far beyond that original notion, and *The New York Times* even once stated, "Dumpstaphunk is the best funk band from New Orleans right now." *Rolling Stone* added, "Dumpstaphunk has grown from a small side project into one of New Orleans's most prestigious modern funk ensembles." Alison Fensterstock, *the* music critic of New Orleans, waxed emphatically: "Dumpstaphunk's groove is a unique monster. It's not the minimalist funk of The Meters and it's not the relentless funk of James Brown, although it has that rhythmic drive. It's not the psychedelic, over-the-top circus of Parliament Funkadelic, but it often has that political slant. It's not the party funk of the Ohio Players, but it shares the high vocals that take the pressure off the bottom. Dumpstaphunk is a whole other school of funk. If you're under 35, you think you've seen funk, but you haven't. You missed the original Meters, James Brown when he wasn't a parody, Parliament Funkadelic's landing of the Mothership, Sly and the Family Stone before he went M.I.A., and Booker T. and the M.G.s before the demise of Stax. Dumpstaphunk is as good as all that, and they're in their prime now."

Dumpstaphunk will be at most large festivals from Jazz & Heritage Festival to Voodoo Music + Arts Experience, and when they're in town, they can be caught performing at their dad's old haunt, Tipitina's.

Deacon John

It's possible that Deacon John may well be the hardest working and most underappreciated musician in New Orleans today. He gleefully plays the blues, R&B, and rock and roll, as a singer, musician, and bandleader. He also acts, having appeared in the horror film *Angel Heart* in 1987 and again 25 years later in another horror film, *The Last Exorcism Part II.*

He's been active in New Orleans's R&B scene since he was a teenager, playing in sessions with Allen Toussaint, Irma Thomas, Lee Dorsey, Ernie K-Doe, the Neville Brothers, and others. He will play anything: R&B, rock, jazz, gospel, soul, and disco, whatever the people want to hear, and he's played everywhere in New Orleans, including stints in the house band at the legendary Dew Drop Inn on LaSalle Street. He has worked as a studio session player, and he's been the man with the band at many weddings (including the weddings of a number of couples, then the weddings of those couples' children, and then the weddings of their grandchildren!).

Deacon John Moore has accepted his place in the New Orleans music scene. He said on NPR: "I never had a hit record, and I never been on tour, and I never played in all these foreign countries. Many of my contemporaries have. I'm just one of the guys who stayed around here and made a living playing music."

Ernie K-Doe

The never shy Ernie K-Doe was been waiting patiently to be the final word in the chapter. And he will not be denied.

Ernie K-Doe was a one-hit wonder, but is also a lifetime of wonderment. Even in New Orleans, where eccentrics are cherished more than merely accepted, K-Doe was in a class by himself. He loved to talk, mostly about himself in a manically, self-aggrandizing way. When he labeled himself "The Emperor of the Universe" no tongue was shoved into his cheek.

Ben Sandmel's biography, *Ernie K-Doe: The R&B Emperor of New Orleans* (The Historic New Orleans Collective, 2012), is as energetic as the man. The book is filled with K-Doe quotes, such as when he described his birth. Ernie waxed, "On the second month, the 22nd day of 19 and 36, at 8:15 in the morning, a boy child was born. Charity Hospital went to rumbling, went to grumbling, start to bending and did all them things. And the doctor said 'What's wrong? What's happening?' The people told them doctors, 'A boy-child is being born on the third floor, at this particular time!' And I believe about that time the doctor had done finished what he had to do, and the nurses had done washed this beautiful body of mines down and brought it to my mother, and I believe my mother looked up at my father and said, 'Huh! What we gonna name the boy this morning?' And my father looked down at my mother and said, 'Hush! You can't name him nothin' but one thing, that's Ernie K-Doe Jr., and he's gonna be a bad motor scooter!'"

Ernie began recording when he was 15 years old. Ten years later, his song "Mother-in-Law" was the first #1 Billboard hit recorded in New Orleans. The song was a tribute to his real-life mother-in-law. He said, "Her name was Lucy. Should have been Lucifer." He'd tell anybody listening that there are only two songs to stand the test of time: "One of them is 'The Star-Spangled Banner.' The other one is 'Mother-in-Law.'" Again, no tongue was planted in any cheek.

He had a few more hits with "A Certain Girl," "T'aint It the Truth," "Come on Home," and "Te-Ta-Te-Ta-Ta." But with the British invasion of the American music scene, K-Doe's style took a back seat to groups like The Rolling Stones with rock and roll stylings that borrowed and stole much from the American R&B sound. Ernie stopped making records and ceased to appear at local clubs. For a while he drank heavily and lived on the streets below the I-10 overpass along Claiborne Avenue.

K-Doe made a comeback of sorts in the 1980s thanks to the efforts of David Freedman, the station manager of WWOZ radio. Freedman gave K-Doe his own rambling and offbeat radio show, broadcast from a low-wattage studio located in the beer storage room upstairs over Tipitina's. Some DJs would drop a microphone

through a hole in the floor to transmit live performances on Tipitina's stage. Fueled by an abundance of ego and alcohol, K-Doe would assault the airwaves with rants about anything that popped into his head.

Freedman characterized the show, "You never knew what the next thing was going to be out of this guy's mouth. It was like he was in a trance state. You had to kind of enter into it, and then as you began to enter into that crazy universe, you'd just kind of surrender to it and it all made sense."

K-Doe's often repeated on-air signature lines included,

"I'm so slick, grease gotta come ask me how to be greasy!"

"I'm so bad I got to pinch myself in the morning to see if I'm still alive!"

"They're fixin' to put my picture on a box of Wheaties!"

"I'm ready to accept the Nobel Prize!"

"There have only been five great singers of rhythm and blues—Ernie K-Doe, James Brown, and Ernie K-Doe!"

And of his radio show, he said:

"Talkin' makes a radio station . . . You must talk. There ain't nobody knowed nothin' about no WWOZ radio station before I come on here . . . But I'm here today!"

When the financially strapped Nora Blatch Educational Foundation had to sell WWOZ to the Jazz Heritage Foundation, new management was less enamored by Ernie K-Doe's on-air stream of semi-consciousness. He was again on the streets.

But this time he was quickly swept up by old friend Antoinette Dorsey Fox, who would later become his second wife. Antoinette clearly had visions for how K-Doe would create his next act. She made him flashy, attention-grabbing outfits and opened the Mother-in-Law Lounge mere yards from where he used to camp out as a homeless person.

Ernie K-Doe died in 2001 at the age of 65 of liver and kidney failure. Antoinette commissioned a life-size mannequin made of K-Doe by artist Jason Poirier. Antoinette often planted the statue on stage in the club so that people could take pictures with the plaster rendition of the late singer. But she would sometimes take the statue out on the town where it might join her at a table inside Galatoire's, ride in parades, and even make a rare appearance at church. The K-Doe mannequin also rode along in a mule-drawn hearse with the procession at Antoinette's funeral when she died in 2009, in a sense making K-Doe the first man ever to attend his own widow's funeral.

Kermit's Mother-in-Law Lounge

1500 N. Claiborne Ave.

Phone: 504-947-1078

Like the juke joint it is, four phone numbers are posted online. Three didn't ring through. The fourth answered with a recorded voice saying, "What's the case Ace? No one can take your call."

Antoinette Dorsey Fox, wife of Ernie K-Doe, opened the club in 1996 as a home for and tribute to her husband. Antoinette made him flashy outfits with shiny suits, feathered hats, and floor-length capes. The club was crowded to the rafters with wall-to-wall photographs and paintings of Ernie K-Doe and a jukebox filled with K-Doe songs. A resplendent Ernie K-Doe himself would greet customers at the door and pose for photographs in the pre-selfie era.

It was a hoppin' place. Eva Perry, a K-Doe backup singer recalled, "I forget how many people it holds, but it used to be wall-to-wall—it was packed. He had people coming from everywhere to hear him."

The juke joint was bought by star trumpet player, Kermit Ruffins, and reopened as Kermit's Mother-in-Law Lounge. When Kermit saw Ernie K-Doe's mannequin he said, "That's gotta go." Sadly, no one seems to know where this eccentric piece of history currently resides. But the lounge itself, located in a somewhat ramshackle neighborhood, is impossible to miss. Look for the large extravagantly painted murals of K-Doe on the exterior.

Kermit Ruffins himself plays there most Sunday nights.

The Importance of Being Stanton

The same way visitors flock to New Orleans to eat our Cajun and Creole food, many people come here to seek out traditional jazz. However, to be a relevant food capital and not a culinary theme park or museum, the city needs new and expansive chefs like Phillip Lopez, Ryan Prewitt, and Alon Shaya. For our music, I'll borrow (steal) a catchphrase from WWOZ radio. To serve as "Guardians of the Groove," New Orleans needs places like Preservation Hall, the Palm Court, and the decks of the Steamboat Natchez to keep the traditional New Orleans jazz sound alive. But to remain a musical hub, we need musicians like Stanton Moore. Without improvisation and expansion, New Orleans music might eventually be no sexier than a corseted 75-year-old Tom Jones singing "What's New Pussycat" . . . again.

Stanton Moore was born and raised in the New Orleans area and was educated at Loyola University on St. Charles Avenue. These facts are important because they secure him as a key figure in the evolution of the city's music. New Orleans is a 300-year-old town with deep roots. Ask any owner of an antebellum mansion in Uptown or the Garden District. Whether they've lived in their house two years or thirty, it's never really "their" house. Others will say, "Oh, you live in the Culpepper house," or "the Beauregard house," or the name of whomever was the original owner.

This provincialism has ramped up since Hurricane Katrina. The city is absorbing waves of YURPs, Young Urban Rebuilding Professionals, who left careers or graduate schools elsewhere to come to New Orleans and be a part of the rebirth process. Some see this as bringing New Orleans a new energy. For others, all these transplants bring the specter of gentrification, the threat of the Best Buy and Foot Locker blandness, or, worst of all, hipsterism.

New Orleanians don't want their bitter hit of chickory coffee replaced by half-caf caramel frappuccino light. Nor do they want their neighborhood juke joints to give way to DJ clubs that blare the latest from Skrillex and Deadmau5.

This attitude of long-term residents bestowing what is legit New Orleans, and what's not, has been termed "NOLA-ier Than Thou." In this regard, some of our best current musicians like Oregonian, Meschiya Lake (voted New Orleans's Best Female Vocalist 2012, 2013, 2014, and 2015), or Belgium-born Helen Gillet would fall short of being in the NOLA-ier Than Thou category.

All that said, Stanton Moore is quintessential New Orleans. In an interview, he recalled, "My mom took me to Mardi Gras parades starting when I was 8 months old. So, around the age of 3, 4, 5, I started really being impacted by the sound of the marching bands coming down the street. By the time I was 6 or 7, I was hitting on stuff in the house—pots and pans, really whatever I could get my hands on. And by the time I was 9 years old, I knew I wanted to be a professional drummer. Now I travel the world playing music that is heavily entrenched in the musical traditions of New Orleans. What's so exciting to me is that I come home eager to go out and see all of my favorite musicians here in town. Guys like Shannon Powell, Herlin Riley, Johnny Vidacovich, Russell Batiste. I draw inspiration from these guys and get excited in the same way I did when I was a kid. Everything I do and see in this city, all that I listen to and participate in, are sources of inspiration and influence, and I continue to incorporate those things into my drumming and my music and continue to take it back out to the world. The musical heritage runs so deep here I'll never get to the end of it. This city is a neverending well of inspiration."

Moore has played, composed, or collaborated with other musicians on virtually every style of music, and has always done so with a New Orleans sensibility. He has played funk, soul, R&B, hip hop, bounce, Mardi Gras carnival music, electronica, straight ahead jazz, even heavy metal—pretty much everything except Tuvan throat singing.

Over a 20-year career, Moore has recorded solo albums, beginning with *All Kooked Out!* (1998), *Flyin' the Koop*, and *III*. He has been a part of noted jazz trios, Garage a Trois (with four albums), Mysteryfunk, Emphasis!, Outre Mer, Power Patriot, the Stanton Moore Trio (which performs regular gigs on Tuesday nights at Snug Harbor), and an all-star band called the Midnite Disturbers. The Midnite Disturbers feature iconic performers like Trombone Shorty and Jamelle Williams on trumpets, Big Sam and Mark Mullins on trombones, Ben Ellman and Skerik on saxophones, Jeffery Hills on sousaphone, and Kevin O'Day with Moore on drums. He still works with all of these acts, plus he does ongoing collaborations with bands such as Dragon Smoke and MG5.

Moore considers his various groups as his diversified portfolio. But his unquestionable blue chip stock is a band called Galactic. For me, personally, Galactic is way beyond blue chip. They have replaced the Talking Heads as my all-time #1 favorite band. Similar to the way in which Talking Heads' frontman, David Byrne, has collaborated with "everyone" from Brian Eno, Richard Thompson, Devo, Arcade Fire, and St. Vincent to create "every" manner of music from post-punk or new wave to mambo, cha-cha, and operatic arias with string arrangements, Stanton Moore has fearlessly joined forces with a great variety of performers to pull, poke, and prod the New Orleans sound into fresh and inventive directions.

Galactic has been called "a hybrid of jazz, funk, blues, R&B, rock, and a horn section to die for, and the band is a perfect representation of what New Orleans can do for a musical soul." Their first album, *Coolin' Off*, released in 1996, was widely acclaimed and propelled the band onto an intense tour schedule. They played more than 200 nights a year for the next 10 years. When I sat down with Moore, he had just returned from Brazil the night before and was flying out to Seattle the next day. Galactic's two follow-up albums, *Ya-Ka-May* and *Carnivale Electricos*, were built upon local New Orleans R&B and the Mardi Gras carnival style. Their fourth album, *From the Corner to the Block*, was heavily influenced by hip hop and used rappers in place of singers.

The five official Galactic members—Stanton Moore, bassist Robert Mercurio, keyboardist Rich Vogel, guitarist Jeff Raines, and saxophonist Ben Ellman—have been together more than two decades. The original vocalist, Theryl DeClouet, left the band in 2004, and ever since they've been what Moore has called "an instrumental band in search of a singer."

These singers include artists who couldn't be more diverse. Contributors include several

stars who are New Orleans locals: Cyril Neville, Maggie Koerner, David Shaw of the Revivalists, Bounce superstar Big Freedia, and rap queen Cheeky Blakk. (Blakk repeats a two-word phrase on the song "Do It Again" that I dare not write here or *Hear Dat* would be a banned book in several states.) Galactic has featured non-New Orleanians like British New Wave singer Joe Jackson, who sometimes tosses a little reggae or old-style swing into his music; LA rapper Chali 2na of Jurassic 5; the hard-driving former lead singer for Living Colour, Corey Glover; and the calming, raspy voiced Grammy-winning R&B, jazz, and soul singer, Macy Gray. DeClouet also rejoins the band on rare occasion. Currently much-admired jazz and soul singer Erica Falls does most of the live shows.

  Instrumentally, Galactic has merged their music with members of the Soul Rebels, the Neville Brothers, the Dirty Dozen Brass Band, George Porter Jr. of The Meters, Skerik, a noted saxophone player from Seattle, and the legendary Allen Toussaint, whose session with the group Moore called, "pretty mind-blowing." Between the time I write this and when *Hear Dat* is published, Stanton will have performed with his number one and dreamed-for collaborator, Maceo Parker, the legendary funk and soul jazz saxophonist, best known for his work with James Brown.

  Not many of us get to live the dreams of our childhood. (I certainly did not become a middle linebacker for the Cleveland Browns.) But Stanton Moore does get to live this dream. Since he was in kindergarten, Stanton Moore wanted to be a drummer. He became just that and he remains head over heels in love with the music of New Orleans. For the last 20 years, he has been much more than a drummer. He joins John Bonham (Led Zeppelin), Neil Peart (Rush), and Ginger Baker (Cream) on *Rolling Stones*'s list of the 50 Greatest Drummers of All Time. For the last 20 years, Stanton Moore has traveled the globe. He has been all over the United States, and I mean all over, including Victor, Idaho; Blackstock, South Carolina; and Thornville, Ohio (I grew up in Ohio, and before writing this piece I had never heard of Thornville). Galactic has traveled the world: Italy, Brazil, France, Japan, Australia, the UK, Netherlands, and Germany. Wherever he travels, he spreads the gospel and the groove of New Orleans music. More than a mere advocate, Stanton Moore is an apostle.

CHAPTER 6

Looking for **Verve** in All the
Wrong Places
(Cajun, Zydeco, and Swamp Pop)

I'm walkin' to New Orleans. I'm gonna need two pair of shoes.

—**Bobby Charles**

A large number of visitors come to New Orleans each year wanting to hear live Cajun music and high-energy zydeco. Hearing recorded music is no problem. It'll be blaring from every T-shirt, Mardi Gras bead, and dried alligator head tourist shop on Decatur Street. Live music is a different story. Now, I didn't live here back in the early '90s when Buckwheat Zydeco was first bringing zydeco to national attention, appearing on TV and performing nationwide as the red-hot warmup band at Eric Clapton and U2 concerts. Maybe it's possible there was a time you could hear the music any night of the week in a variety of clubs. Instead, I think tourists' misplaced hunger for Cajun and zydeco music was created by the popular movie, *The Big Easy* (1986). Viewers were subjected to the worst attempt at a New Orleans accent in the history of film. Dennis Quaid's character, Remy McSwain, dropped a slathering of "chers" into each sentence the way teenagers fill in with "likes." The movie also, like, created the false notion that crawfish boils and Cajun dances were as ubiquitous in New Orleans as, like, Starbucks.

Oh, cher, they are not. You have to travel a good two to three hours outside the city, to Mamou or Opelousas in the heart of Cajun country, for that kind of experience. Cajuns were the displaced French Canadians who refused to sign an oath to the English king. They were trappers and farmers. They were country folk and not destined for the Big City, even one as laid back as New Orleans. If you do a road trip out into Cajun Country, a stop at Fred's Lounge in Mamou is a must. Fred's has been airing live radio broadcasts every Saturday morning since 1962. The music will be loud, raucous, and sung 100 percent in French. If you don't arrive before 8:30 a.m., there won't be any place to sit. An hour later, there won't be any place to stand. And there's a rule at Fred's: Once you enter you don't get to leave until you dance.

Cajun music is rooted in French ballads. It's a waltzin' and a dancin' music, and it uses only a few instruments like the Cajun accordion, fiddle, and triangle. Zydeco is the Creole-influenced cousin of Cajun music, with some blues and R&B mixed in, and uses the accordion (squeeze box) and frottoir (washboard). These styles share common musical origins and influences, and an oversimplification would be to say that Cajun is the music of the white Acadians of South Louisiana, and zydeco is the music of the black Creoles of the same region.

Now, I don't mean to make it sound like finding this music is impossible. You *can* listen to Cajun and zydeco musicians in New Orleans, you just have to work a little bit.

David Doucet, former member of the multi–Grammy-Award-winning Beau-Soleil, performs every Monday night at The Columns Hotel. He is joined in the elegant setting by bassist Al Tharp in guitar/fiddle duets.

For the last 25 years, Tipitina's has hosted a weekly Fais Do Do every Sunday, where Bruce Daigrepont and his button accordion have played more than 1,000 shows.

A Fais Do Do is the traditional name for a home dance party in Cajun country. Mothers would take their young children to a separate "Cry Room" and gently encourage them to go to sleep (Do Do) so they could get back to the dance floor.

The restaurant Mulate's plays Cajun music right across the street from the Convention Center every night after 7:00 p.m. The original Mulate's is located in the town of Beaux Bridge (two hours from New Orleans) and featured the great Zachary Richard as their opening night performer, followed by Richard and Michael Doucet of BeauSoleil, and classic old-timers such as Hector Duhon and Octa Clark. Stars Paul Simon and Joe Cocker have shared the stage at Mulate's. Since establishing a location in New Orleans, Mulate's has become a bit of a tourist trap with just okay Cajun food and resident bands that are likewise . . . just okay.

Amanda Shaw

Amanda Shaw is the darling of the current New Orleans Cajun music scene. She's been playing the Cajun fiddle and singing since she was 8 years old. *The Rosie O'Donnell Show* gave Amanda her first national exposure when she was in grade school. Now in her mid-20s, Amanda is probably still carded in most clubs where she plays. I once witnessed two not-so-young clerks at Louisiana Music Factory get all silly-flustered like high school freshmen when she came in and actually talked to them.

Amanda Shaw   George Berkis

Amanda and her band, the Cute Guys, perform at state fairs, Andouille Festivals (andouille is a type of smoked sausage that originated in France), appear with some frequency at the Rock 'n' Bowl, and perform every year at Jazz & Heritage Festival. They've cut four albums, which are a mix of traditional Cajun dancehall standards with Cajun'd-up covers of songs like "Should I Stay or Should I Go," by the Clash, and "I Wanna Be Your Boyfriend," by the Ramones.

Zydeco

The commonly held explanation for the term *zydeco* is that it comes from the Creole saying, "Les haricots song pas salés," which means, "The beans aren't salty." Haricots (string beans) is pronounced "zah ree' co." Maybe the music had been played during the bean-harvesting season. Regardless, little by little, "zah ree' co" evolved into zydeco.

Clifton Chenier

The undisputed king of zydeco is Clifton Chenier. He ain't New Orleans. Chenier was born in Opelousas, died in Lafayette, and took with him a Grammy Award and a National Heritage Fellowship. He was inducted into the Blues Hall of Fame and the Louisiana Music Hall of Fame, and in 2014 he was a posthumous recipient of the Grammy Lifetime Achievement Award.

His musical heirs are likewise fixtures in the rural Louisiana zydeco scene. They include Chris Ardoin and Boozoo Chaviz (Lake Charles), John Delafose (Eunice), Wayne Toups (Lafayette), and Rosie Ledet (Church Point).

John Delafose

John Delafose's son Geno played rubboard with his dad's band, switching to accordion after his father's death. His music has been classified "nouveau zydeco" because he mixes in a little country and western.

Rockin' Dopsie Jr.

Also following in his father's footsteps is Rockin' Dopsie Jr. When the original Rockin' Dopsie, called the James Brown of zydeco, unexpectedly passed away in 1993, the son vowed to keep his memory alive with his incarnation of the band, Rockin' Dopsie Jr. & The Zydeco Twisters. The Zydeco Twisters are the only band fronted (flamboyantly) by a washboard player in place of the accordionist or guitarist.

Nate Williams Jr.

Nate Williams Jr. doesn't follow in his father's footsteps, but right alongside them. Both his band, Lil' Nathan & the Zydeco Big Timers, and his dad's band, Nathan & the Zydeco Cha-Chas, alternate gigs at the Rock 'n' Bowl. Both bands play regularly on the road.

Chubby Carrier

Chubby Carrier is a third-generation zydeco artist with Louisiana famous relatives, Roy Carrier (father), Warren Carrier (grandfather), and cousins Bebe and Calvin Carrier. All are considered legends in zydeco. Chubby began his musical career at the age of 12 by playing drums with his father's band. He began playing the accordion at the age of 15, formed his own band in 1989, has recorded 10 CDs, and picked up a Grammy Award for the 2011 album, *Zydeco Junkie*.

Sunpie Barnes & the Louisiana Sunspots

The music of Sunpie Barnes & the Louisiana Sunspots is not pure zydeco. Their music, termed "Bouje Bouje" has its own twists and turns, stirring zydeco with heavier doses of Caribbean and West African music. Sunpie's personal history has as many twists and turns. He's been a park ranger, an actor, former high school biology teacher, former college football All-American, and former NFL player (Kansas City Chiefs). He is Second Chief of the North Side Skull and Bone Gang, one of the oldest existing carnival groups in New Orleans, and a member of the Black Men of Labor Social Aid and Pleasure Club. Musically, Sunpie Barnes plays the piano, percussion, harmonica, and accordion.

Sunpie & the Louisiana Sunspots play regularly way uptown at Dos Jefes (5535 Tchoupitoulas St.), a cigar bar with fine wine and spirits and live music.

Swamp Pop

Another Louisiana music style not-so-much a part of New Orleans heritage is swamp pop. It's a music born in the Acadiana region of south Louisiana and southeast Texas, where teenagers swapped their parents' fiddles and accordions for electric guitars to create a regional interpretation of rock 'n' roll. Johnnie Allan is called the "King of Swamp Pop" for his many hits that include "Lonely Days and Lonely Nights," a virtual swamp pop anthem. In a story for *Louisiana Soundtrack*, a publication by the Louisiana Office of Tourism, Johnnie recalled the early days: "Rod Bernard, Warren Storm, Tommy McClain, Clint West, and I started recording this music in the late 1950s and early 1960s, not realizing that we were creating a new genre of music. It was called swamp pop in the 1970s by a guy from England named Bill Millar. We just called it south Louisiana music." Allan also quickly dismisses his moniker as "King" adding, "I don't go around wearing a crown."

Many swamp pop songs hit the Billboard charts, including 'Walkin' to New Orleans," "Running Bear," "Sea of Love," "Mathilda, I'm Leaving It Up to You," "Before the Next Teardrop Falls," and "Stop and Think It Over." There is now a Swamp Pop Music Festival in Gonzales (an hour outside New Orleans) and a Swamp Pop Museum in Ville Platte (two-and-a-half hours away). The museum is housed in a restored Southern Pacific train depot.

The best locally available taste of swamp pop is the Grammy-nominated Creole String Beans, yet another band that graces the Rock 'n' Bowl stage. They call themselves "Y'at Rock," and on their website they declare, "The band's mission has been to keep the great indigenous music of New Orleans and South Louisiana alive in a live context; to keep the dancers sweating on the floor and the listeners smiling behind their beers."

The Radiators, after 33 years of performing, have sadly sort of called it quits. Their website alludes to a possible but not probable reunion. "We will keep ya'll posted about any other Rads stuff." The same five band members had remained together since they formed in 1978. They called their version of swamp rock "Fish-head music." The Radiators flirted with success. Their first record, *Law of the Fish,* made it to #139 on the Billboard charts. The next album got to #122. The failure to crack the Top 100 ensured that record labels would be only too supportive of their return to what they did best—live performances. The Radiators were known for massive, marathon-length concerts where their funky dance beats would go on five hours or more. They were the #1 favorite band for several generations of Tulane students, though their once-a-week gig, every Wednesday night at Luigi's Pizza Parlor, was literally cut off when a band member brought in a real chainsaw during a performance of their song "Texas Chainsaw Massacre."

SPOTLIGHT

Rock 'n' Bowl
3000 S. Carrollton Ave.
Phone: 504-861-1700

The spot whose calendar is most filled with zydeco, cajun, and swamp pop music is the Rock 'n' Bowl. It is a bar, bowling alley, and music hall all rolled into one. It's like an amusement park for people that like to drink and dance (and bowl).

When it's zydeco night at the Rock 'n' Bowl, all the country boys come into the Big City to dance. And by "boys" I mean 70-year-old men with more moves than teeth. There is nothing creepy nor salacious about the boys, but they will line up in front of the purdy ladies and one after another after another wait for the last feller to finish his spin and then respectfully ask, "May I dance with you Ma'am?" Back in the '90s, when my wife was only a few years from leaving her career as a stage and cabaret performer, she begged me to get her out the front door. Them old guys done wore her out.

And in 2000, when my afternoon wedding started to wind down and Kermit Ruffins had left the premises, we grabbed our wedding party and friends and ran out to the Rock 'n' Bowl. I bowled an alcohol-impaired 63. Having experienced the Rock 'n' Bowl for the first time that night, my cousin Margot was married there a year later.

Dr. John

CHAPTER 7

We're All in the **Mood** for a **Revery** and They Got Us **Feeling Alright** (The Piano Men of New Orleans)

The piano ain't got no wrong notes. —**Thelonious Monk**

New Orleans has a long and glorious musical history. And it may have the funkiest history of the best piano men anywhere. It goes all the way back to Louis Moreau Gottschalk. Born in 1829, Gottschalk absorbed both the music of African slaves and the European art music he heard throughout his native New Orleans. Even though he was sent to Paris at age 12 for a formal music education, his adult compositions held on to that New Orleans sound by way of Latin rhythms and the rolling right hand. He composed some proto-ragtime work that predates Scott Joplin by a good 50 years. A lot of what he wrote is now considered pure kitsch, but back in his day he was a cult figure, admired as a pianist by serious composers Chopin, Berlioz, and much of the musical cognoscenti. Gottschalk's most enduring song is "Bamboula, Opus 2," which was quite revolutionary at the time.

In the late 1700s, a visiting Spanish bishop to New Orleans was appalled by the slave dances, calling them "the wicked custom of the negroes, who, at the hour of Vespers, assemble in an expanse called Place Congo to dance the bamboula and perform hideous gyrations." Some 50 years later, a Paris newspaper announced a new tune that "everyone in Europe knows, Bamboula, thanks to Louis Moreau Gottschalk, the New Orleans pianist-composer, who has brought a host of curious chants from the Creoles and the Negroes; he has made from them the themes of his most delicious compositions."

Some of New Orleans's greatest piano men have already been covered elsewhere in this book. Professor Longhair was in the R&B and Funk chapter. Allen Toussaint was the subject of the Overture at the beginning of this book. That still leaves a great many New Orleans piano masters.

Tuts Washington

Isadore "Tuts" Washington was one of the original New Orleans piano masters. His musical roots go back to turn-of-the-century Storyville. He was born in 1907 and was raised by an aunt who enthusiastically encouraged his musical talents. Tuts was all a-tingle over the barrelhouse style, but his aunt was determined that he should have a wider repertoire, so he also learned to play pop, jazz, boogie, and ragtime.

Tuts only recorded one album. It was a mixture of jazz standards and low-down blues plus vocals on one risqué song, "Papa Yellow Blues." This tune gave Tuts his other nickname, Papa Yellow. His nonrecorded work practically defined New Orleans music, and Tuts is claimed to have been a major influence on all the greats who followed: Fats Domino, Professor Longhair, James Booker, Dr. John, and Allen Toussaint.

Tuts Washington is also famous for exemplifying the tired old cliché, "He died doing what he loved," because he did just that in the middle of a performance at the 1984 New Orleans World's Fair.

James Booker

If you want to praise James Booker, called "the Black Liberace" and "the Bayou Maharajah," get in line. Practically every other important piano man of New Orleans has waxed poetic while worshipping at the altar of James Booker.

Allen Toussaint had said, "Genius is a word that is thrown around so loosely, but let me say that if the word is applicable to anyone, the person who comes to mind is James Booker. Total genius. Within all the romping and stomping in his music, there were complexities in it that were supported by some extreme technical acrobatics finger-wise that made his music extraordinary."

Josh Paxton elaborates, "It's Ray Charles on the level of Chopin. It's all the soul, all the groove, and all the technique in the universe packed into one unbelievable player. It's like playing Liszt and Professor Longhair at the same time. I can now say with certainty that it's a pianistic experience unlike any other. He invented an entirely new way of playing blues and roots-based music on the piano, and it was mind-blowingly brilliant and beautiful."

Harry Connick Jr. called him "a powerful genius of a unique and complex mind. I hear joy and struggle. I hear perfection and error. I hear confidence and hesitation—I hear James Booker, the greatest ever."

Arthur Rubenstein, considered one of the greatest classical pianists of the 20th century, was in New Orleans on tour. After his concert, Rubinstein was introduced to an 18-year-old Booker who played several tunes for him. Rubenstein was astonished, saying, "I could never play that . . . never at that tempo."

Dr. John playfully described Booker as "the best black, gay, one-eyed junkie piano genius New Orleans has ever produced."

In other words, no one has ever played the piano like Booker. Current piano master Tom McDermott notes that "Booker's music has mystery. The mystery of where he got his ideas, but also the notes themselves. I've listened for thousands of hours, and could only figure out so much. There are still things I can't decipher, over 30 years after I've first heard them."

In spite of all his current adulation, Booker never gained huge fame in America while alive, but he did in France and Germany. Some feel it was Europe's lesser racism and homophobia that opened doors. Returning to New Orleans, Booker was devastated by the reduced notoriety he received back home. He took to playing house piano at the Maple Leaf and other small bars.

He died at the age of 43 while seated in a wheelchair in the emergency room at New Orleans's Charity Hospital, waiting to receive medical attention.

Huey "Piano" Smith

An important if lesser-known part of the great New Orleans piano tradition is Huey "Piano" Smith. He stumbled in and out the footsteps of Professor Longhair and Fats Domino, as his taste ran toward the comedic, often with complete nonsense for lyrics.

At age 15, Huey Smith backed New Orleans legends Earl King and Guitar Slim and quickly became a popular session pianist, playing on records by the top R&B musicians, including Smiley Lewis ("I Hear You Knockin'"), Lloyd Price ("Stagger Lee"), and the oft-visiting Little Richard ("Tutti Frutti"). During the mid-'50s, Smith created his own band, the Clowns, which usually featured popular blues singer and female impersonator Bobby Marchan. His breakout almost came in 1959 with the to-be nationwide hit, "Sea Cruise." However, the Ace record label chose to have a white teenage singer, Frankie Ford, overdub Huey's vocals.

At his peak, Smith epitomized New Orleans R&B at its most infectious and rollicking best. This is exemplified by his classic tune, "Rockin' Pneumonia and the Boogie Woogie Flu." Unable to break through to the charts, Piano did the unthinkable. He left the music industry permanently and became a Jehovah's Witness.

Fats Domino

Fats Domino's pianos are all over town. His all-white piano is in the Jazz Museum, along with Louis Armstrong's first trumpet, located inside the U.S. Mint just past the French Market. A waterlogged piano, recovered from his Ninth Ward house and recording studio after Hurricane Katrina, is on display at The Cabildo museum at the back of Jackson Square.

Fats sold more than 65 million records over his career. He had 37 top-40 hits. Only Elvis sold more records over the same time period. His Billboard hits include "Blue Monday," "Blueberry Hill," "I'm Ready," "Ain't That a Shame," and "Walking to New Orleans." He was awarded the Grammy Lifetime Achievement Award and was part of the Rock and Roll Hall of Fame's inaugural class in 1986.

Many consider Fats the father of R&B, and some feel that his single "The Fat Man" is the earliest rock 'n' roll song. That spirited single hit the Billboard chart on April Fool's Day in 1950.

Fats now lives in Harvey on the West Bank. He stopped performing after his 2007 farewell concert in Tipitina's. He neither tours nor travels. When he was awarded the National Medal of Arts, he turned down President Clinton's invitation to accept it at the White House, commenting, "I traveled so much, I don't have anywhere left to go."

Dr. John

Dr. John's, more properly Mac Rebbenack's, personal story reads like an episodic 19th-century novel or the script for a Coen brothers movie. It's filled with twists and turns, good and evil, highs and lows, but always with a twinkle in the eye. He wrote a memoir himself, *Under a Hoodoo Moon*, which is superb reading.

His music education is sort of a street hustler's guide to success. Dr. John had next to no formal education. As a kid he joined a choir, but got kicked out.

Mac used to accompany his father on one of his side jobs, supplying records to second-rate hotels. His dad would drop off blues, jazz, and what was then called race records, and pick up overly used ones. Mac got to keep all the ones considered too scratchy, and he started mimicking the style he heard on the records he played.

Leonard James was his next musical father figure. James would get him gigs at strip joints, shake dances, brothels, grocery stores, department stores, anywhere that would have him. He was 13 at the time. He played what they call "jiffy jobs." A band would be booked for 12-hour sets with no breaks. When a band member had to take a break, go to the bathroom or eat, the young Mac would jump in and cover his instrument.

Professor Longhair turned out to be his streetwise spirit guide and corner stoop Yoda. Mac was working a gig with Roy Brown's band when Longhair came by one night and said he needed a band. Mac's whole band up and quit without notice and went out the door with the local hero.

The Professor taught Mac about technique. In Dr. John's own unique style of talking, revealed in a *BOMB Magazine* interview, he described his interactions with Professor Longhair: "He and his vibe were so hip that I was just magnetized to the cat, you know? I asked him, 'Wow, what are you doin' when you're doin' all the stuff like that?' And he said, 'That's double-note crossovers.' And I said, 'Well, what is that stuff when I see your hands going all over?' And he says, 'Over and unders.' He had names for everything. He'd say things to his band guys, like, this oola-mala-walla stuff, and I thought, Wow, this guy's speakin' in tongues." Longhair also taught him respect for the music. "If you played music for the money, you wasn't gonna be a good musician. But if you played music for lovin' the music, at least you cared about that. It was a major thing, because it connected with my livelihood, you know?"

The Professor's one unlearned lesson was about drugs. Fess, said Dr. John, "used to tell you what you were doin', includin' messing with that other shit so you wouldn't be a disaster. One thing you gotta learn is, if you smoke weed, it ain't so bad; but if you shoot dope, it's gonna fuck everything."

Dr. John has had a tumultuous career with a decades-long heroin addiction. During the 1950s, he sold narcotics and ran a brothel. He was arrested on drug charges and sentenced to two years in a federal prison at Fort Worth, Texas.

Over the last 25 years, he has cleaned up, or at least cut back on his act. In the late 1960s, Rebennack gained fame as a solo artist after creating the persona of Dr. John, The Night Tripper. Dr. John's act combined New Orleans–style rhythm and blues with psychedelic rock and elaborate stage shows that came off like Screamin' Jay Hawkins's act with voodoo religious ceremonies, complete with elaborate costumes and headdress.

A decade later, he'd had enough of what he called "the mighty-coo-de-fiyo hoodoo show" and so dumped the routine in favor of New Orleans standards. He is now worshipped by R&B lovers and is respected by the jazz and rock crowds. Dr. John has six Grammy Awards and as many hit songs that will forever be a part of New Orleans musical heritage: "Right Place Wrong Time," "Gris-Gris Gumbo Ya Ya," "Mama Roux," "I Walk on Guilded Splinters," and "Goin' Back to New Orleans."

Henry Butler

Blind since birth, pianist and vocalist Henry Butler was the bridge between New Orleans R&B of the '60s and the modern McCoy Tyner type of jazz in the post-Coltrane era. Butler always kept traditional New Orleans style as his starting point, but used jazz, Caribbean, classical, pop, blues, and R&B (among others) for his fearless improvisations. *The New York Times* wrote of Butler, "Percussive in his attack, ostentatious with his technique, he was the picture of stubborn mischief."

Eddie Bo

Eddie came from a long line of men who were shipbuilders, bricklayers, carpenters, and masons by day, and musicians by night. He began playing in the New Orleans jazz scene, but made a switch to R&B after deciding it was more popular and would bring him more money. He was prolific, cutting 22 albums and more than 50 singles, which predate his albums.

Like a lot of local musicians, Eddie frequented the premier blues venue in town, Dew Drop Inn on LaSalle Street. He also played at the Club Tijuana under the name of Spider Bocage, later forming the Spider Bocage Orchestra, which toured the country supporting singers Big Joe Turner, Earl King, Guitar Slim, Johnny Adams, Lloyd Price, Ruth Brown, Smiley Lewis, and The Platters.

Joe Krown

A Long Island boy, Joe Krown was drawn to New Orleans in 1992 to join Clarence "Gatemouth" Brown's band. He was the band's keyboard player for 22 years, or until Gatemouth's death. From 1996 to 2001, he held the honor of being the Monday performer for the Traditional Piano Night slot at Maple Leaf Bar. The spot was formerly held by Professor Longhair, and later James Booker.

Krown plays in several different styles. When he plays the piano as a solo artist he typically plays in the traditional New Orleans jazz style. When he plays with his band, the Joe Krown Organ Combo, the sound is funk. And then there's his trio with Johnny Sansone and John Folse that plays an early dinner set at Ralph's On the Park, and then an after-dinner set (9:00–midnight) at the Public Belt inside the Hilton Riverside Hotel. In the spring of 2007, Krown started playing again every Sunday night at the Maple Leaf with Walter "Wolfman" Washington (guitar and vocals) and Russell Batiste Jr. (drums).

He's also played at House of Blues, Tipitina's, Le Bon Temps Roule, d.b.a., and

Funky Butt. To see if Krown is performing while you're in New Orleans, you might want to call any of these joints and ask, "Is Joe playing there tonight?"

Tom McDermott

Growing up in St. Louis, Tom McDermott drank in the ragtime blues there, earned a master's degree in music, and then was sucked into New Orleans by his love for our piano greats, Professor Longhair, James Booker, and Dr. John.

For most of the '90s, he played for the Dukes of Dixieland. He then ventured off on his own to form the Nightcrawlers. He is one of the more educated and eclectic players in New Orleans. He is perhaps the only piano man in town who even knows of Louis Moreau Gottschalk, let alone includes his numbers from the 1800s in his sets. He also loves (and will play) Brazilian choro music, French musette, The Beatles, and early Duke Ellington. When you go to a Tom McDermott show, you sort of have to be ready for anything.

McDermott plays Wednesday nights with Meschiya Lake from 7:00–9:00 p.m. at Chickie Wah Wah's, and on Thursdays he plays an early set (5:00–7:00 p.m.) at Three Muses and a later set at Buffa's on Esplanade. The first Friday of each month, McDermott joins Aurora Nealand at The Bombay Club.

CHAPTER 8

Divas and Crooners

It's just something about the way we, as performers from this city, the way we do things. We hear extra sounds in our heads—extra beats, extra backbeats, extra rhythms that people from other parts of the United States just don't understand or get.

—Irma Thomas

In many cities, a lounge singer or club performer becomes an integral part of their city's identity. In New York City, Bobby Short was the featured icon at The Carlyle hotel for 35 years. In Minneapolis, the legendary Lou Snider (who was my personal icon) held court at Nye's Polonaise Room. Decked out in her leopard-patterned spandex and kitty cat glasses, for nearly 50 years she sat upfront, beneath a smoke-stained portrait of Chopin and took requests. She seemed to know every pop song and show tune ever written. Every time I visited the Twin Cities, going out to hear her sing was mandatory. New Orleans has its share of divas and crooners, too. This chapter will focus on both those who are no longer around and those who are still singing, so that you can hear them, live, while you're here.

Louis Prima

Of those who you can no longer see, Louis Prima may be the best known. He is, however, possibly the least New Orleanian. Yes, he was born here and did start his career in the late '20s with a seven-piece New Orleans–style jazz band called the New Orleans Gang. His brother Leon had a noted spot on Bourbon Street called the 500 Club, and Prima is buried in New Orleans at the Lake Lawn Metairie cemetery. But, in between, his greatest fame and success came in Las Vegas and New York City by way of the non-New Orleanian sounds of swing and big band music. His grave-stone is etched with the lyrics from one of his hits, "Just a Gigolo." Visitors to his site leave pennies on his tomb in honor of another hit song, "Pennies from Heaven."

Lee Dorsey

Irving Lee Dorsey was an R&B fixture on the Billboard charts in the 1960s. His first hit was "Rock Pretty Baby" on Cosimo Matassa's Rex record label. Once Allen Toussaint entered his life, Lee Dorsey cranked out hit songs in rapid succession: "Ya Ya," "Lottie Mo," "Lover of Love," "Ride Your Pony," "Get Out of My Life, Woman," "Holy Cow," and most famously, "Working in the Coal Mine."

Both "Ya Ya" and "Ride Your Pony" reached #7 on the charts. "Coal Mine" is his most enduring hit and has been covered by pretty much everyone, including Devo.

Harry Connick Jr.

You "could" see Harry Connick Jr. in New Orleans, but I highly doubt you will. When not taping *American Idol* in California, Harry and his Victoria's Secret model wife and their (I assume perfect) children now live in New Canaan, Connecticut.

Connick started learning the keyboards at age 3, playing publicly at age 5, and recording with a local jazz band at 10. When he was 9 years old, he performed the Piano Concerto No. 3 Opus 37 of Beethoven with the New Orleans Symphony Orchestra.

Connick's biggest break came when director Rob Reiner asked him to do the music for his movie *When Harry Met Sally*. The soundtrack had him singing (and sounding like Sinatra with a y'at accent) several standards like, "It Had to Be You," "Let's Call the Whole Thing Off," and "Don't Get Around Much Anymore." The album went double-platinum and won him his first Grammy Award for Best Jazz Male Vocal. He's now won three Grammy Awards, two Emmy Awards, and has sold more than 28 million albums, including ten #1 jazz albums, more than any other artist in jazz-chart history.

You can take the boy out of New Orleans and stick him in the Nutmeg State, but you can't take New Orleans out of the boy. As fine a singer and actor as he may be, it's his arrangements that really shine. There's a little New Orleans in everything he does. His *Songs I Heard* is my all-time favorite children's album. He even turns (my much-despised) "Supercalifragilisticexpialidocious" into a hip jazzy tune.

Jeremy Davenport

The Ritz-Carlton spent some $250 million to transform a former department store into a luxury hotel. Their "ritzy" bar and club has become the Davenport Lounge, home to Jeremy Davenport every week, Thursday through Saturday nights.

The jazz singer and trumpeter is from a musical family from St. Louis, and he came to New Orleans to learn from Wynton and Ellis Marsalis. Recognizing his talent (he's been compared to Chet Baker), Harry Connick Jr. scooped him up for his Big Band and took the then-18-year-old Jeremy on the road for six years. Davenport reveled in his role as the band's youngest member and wise-ass kid.

Davenport came back to New Orleans as a solo artist with an absolute passion for the Great American Songbook, namely pop numbers from the 1930s and '40s. Along with his own compositions, he performs crooning versions of "One for My Baby," "Some Day You'll Be Sorry," and "I'm Old-Fashioned." Even when doing well-known standards, Davenport likes to add improvisation and what he calls "authentic" swing.

The Davenport Lounge is the perfect setting for his unique talent. As a confident young artist, however, he expected to be "discovered," and he envisioned a Michael Bublé or Harry Connick Jr. type of career for himself. It was Connick who eventually sat him down, saying, "Bro, you're waiting for something that's never going to happen." Prompted by Connick, he became a regular at Snug Harbor Jazz Bistro and made a series of appearances on Emeril Lagasse's TV shows. He's also been on *The Tonight Show with Jay Leno* and on *The Late Show with David Letterman*. He has also been featured in magazines: *Cosmopolitan, GQ, Travel + Leisure*, and *People*.

John Boutté

John Boutté is a singer you can hear live most every week, most often Saturday nights at d.b.a. His route to stage notoriety was not your usual one. Boutté did play the trumpet and cornet in marching bands in his junior high and high school days, but went on to major in business at Xavier University in New Orleans, spent four years in the military, and then took a job at a credit union when he returned to civilian life.

Boutté was nudged toward a music career by two greats. Danny Barker counseled the young Boutté that his business career didn't have a glass ceiling, so much as it had a brick wall. Boutté also met Stevie Wonder, who recommended he pursue a career in music. Boutté says, "I decided I had to do what was in my heart." He soon joined his sister Lillian on her singing tour of Europe, and his professional singing career started.

Boutté's greatest claim to fame came when the HBO *Treme* series chose a song from his *Jambalaya* album to be the opening theme song. It has since become his standard (or maybe his cross to bear) like "Margaritaville" is for Jimmy Buffet or "Danke Schoen" is for Wayne Newton.

If you do go see John Boutté perform live, please do not shout out the request from the audience. As Boutté concedes, "I know I need to sing it, even when I might feel like singing something else."

Before the night is over, you will get your desired "buck jumping and having fun."

Bobby Lounge

Bobby is not from New Orleans, but comes from McComb, Mississippi. He did not start singing until after his daddy died (Daddy would not have approved), and he had to quit singing for a spell for health reasons. He doesn't play often in New Orleans, but does perform at most every Jazz Fest and has sung at Tipitina's, House of Blues, and the makeshift stage at Louisiana Music Factory. I include him here because if Bobby Lounge is in town, you need you some Bobby Lounge. The *Times-Picayune* newspaper asserted he is best experienced "by the open mind or at least a mind half-clouded with drink."

He takes the stage in an iron lung (don't worry, it's just a prop), accompanied by Nursie (not a real nurse, but a voluptuous model in nurse's wear). Lounge then starts banging on the piano like it insulted his momma. Of his two-fisted playing he has said that "I weed out the inferior instruments." The delight in beholding his performance comes from his spewing eccentric lyrics, like a deep-fried Tom Waits.

Lounge is aware of his own limitations, saying, "I hear wrong notes and I wish my voice sounded better. I am pretty limited. I play everything in C." But his outrageous enthusiasm and his gift for storytelling will blow you away (for three or four songs at least).

Irma Thomas

Irma Thomas was a mother at 14, and four times a mother by 19. She also started to acquire some local notoriety in her job as "The Singing Waitress." She was eventually fired from her restaurant gig because customers kept asking for the singing waitress rather than an omelet and a side of grits. It was time for Irma to go anyway, because she had the fortune to start sitting in with Tommy Ridgley and the Untouchables band at the Pimlico Club in Central City. Ridgley introduced her to Ron Records where she cut her first single in 1959 for what would become the classic, "(You Can Have My Husband) But Don't Mess with My Man."

The dynamic young singer was soon snatched up by Minit Records, where she began recording a series of hit songs written and produced by Allen Toussaint. "Cry On," "I Done Got Over It," "It's Raining," and "Ruler of My Heart" made her a local celebrity. For whatever reason, and a lack of talent was *not* the reason, Irma Thomas never managed to cross over into mainstream popular success like her contemporaries Aretha Franklin, Gladys Knight, and Dionne Warwick.

Thomas abandoned her pursuit of a career in singing and took a day job at a Montgomery Ward department store while she raised her four children as a single mother. In the same way the New Orleans Jazz & Heritage Festival saved Professor Longhair's career, it saved Thomas's. Organizers invited her to perform at the outdoor festival, which led to the revival of her music career. Producer Scott Billington brought Thomas to Rounder Records in the mid-'80s and they produced a string of great albums: *The New Rules, The Way I Feel, Simply the Best, True Believer, Walk Around Heaven, The Story of My Life,* and *Sing It!*

Simply the Best and *Sing It!* both received Grammy nominations. In 2007, she won the Grammy Award for *After the Rain.*

The one-time "singing waitress" is now known as the "Soul Queen of New Orleans."

Boswell Sisters

The Boswell Sisters—Martha, Connie, and Vet—were one of the first celebrity groups to appear on a national scale in the new radio age of the 1920s and '30s. Together they pioneered the cheerful, close-harmony style that became emblematic of the times. The Andrews Sisters would become the quintessential of this style of singing 10 years later. But the Boswell Sisters did pretty well, also. They sold 75 million records.

In his book, *Jazz Singing,* Will Friedwald called the Boswell Sisters "the greatest of all jazz vocal groups." Part of the lore of the Boswell Sisters was that they were completely attuned to one another: They could start singing independently in separate rooms, gravitate toward one another, and find upon meeting that they were not only at the same spot in the same song, in tempo and in key, but in perfect harmony.

If you want to be in a better mood in 2 minutes and 25 seconds, go to YouTube and watch "Crazy People" by the Boswell Sisters.

The Pfister Sisters

Fifty years after the Boswell Sisters, three women from New Orleans who were not really sisters got together to form a group to help out a friend. George Schmidt and his band, the New Leviathan Oriental Foxtrot Orchestra, had been hired to play a private party for some very wealthy and rather unreasonable clients. Their one stipulation was that the music had to be nonstop. To fill the gaps when members of Oriental Foxtrot needed breaks, George asked Holley Bendtsen to perform songs.

Bendtsen agreed, and then recruited two more singers, Suzi Malone and Yvette Voelker, to pitch in. They named the one-night-only group The Pfister Sisters. They learned five songs for the gig, but, from this performance, a long-term institution was born.

They performed at the Jazz & Heritage Festival later that year and have since gotten gigs for their three-part harmony at bars, festivals, and state penitentiaries. They have also sung for foreign dignitaries.

The Pfister Sisters pay homage to the original Boswell Sisters both by covering their songs and by bringing their brassy attitude to the stage.

They can also be seen every Sunday from 2:00–6:00 p.m. at The Spotted Cat.

Debbie Davis

As the daughter of two opera singers, Debbie Davis seemed destined to her career as a singer. She made her first professional singing appearance at age 2. She had a budding reputation as a rock singer in her home state of New Jersey when she moved to New Orleans in 1997. Here, she did a hard left turn into jazz and the Great American Songbook (though she does, now and again, sing covers of songs by Led Zeppelin and The Velvet Underground). Davis has become one of the city's better singers, and is sometimes compared to Miss Peggy Lee for both her hand-on-hip style and her ample appearance. She is also New Orleans's absolute best ukulele player (I can't really name another). She has performed with a wide range of performers, from New Orleans staples like John Boutté and Tom McDermott to a couldn't-be-more-different Soul Asylum and the Misfits. And yes, she is one of the current Pfister Sisters.

Davis plays a variety of clubs, but she can most reliably be found at Three Muses most Saturday nights.

Banu Gibson

Banu Gibson cut her singing teeth in sunny-happy places, working for Jackie Gleason at his Joe the Bartender room in Miami and at Disneyland in California. Then, her husband accepted a job with Tulane University in New Orleans. New Orleans blew its own version of pixie dust over her, which was infused with the soporific scent of humidity, spilled beer, dead moss, frying fat, and discarded crawfish tails. And she's been singing the city's praises ever since.

Gibson told myNewOrleans.com, "What I realized is that every place else in the United States is white bread and mayonnaise, and everything here is not—it's spicy and the architecture is so different. You can't control where you were born, but you have a choice where you live!"

Her music choices remain Great American Songbook standards from the 1920s to '40s. She's one of the few, perhaps the only, New Orleans singers absolutely and exclusively devoted to the classic songs of Gershwin, Duke Ellington, Irving Berlin, Hoagy Carmichael, Cole Porter, and Rodgers and Hart.

If your desire is to hear great renditions of songs like "Top Hat" or "Isn't it Romantic," you need to see which of her venues she's playing tonight. Gibson plays regularly at Snug Harbor, The Bombay Club, Three Muses, and the New Orleans Museum of Art.

Aurora Nealand

Aurora Nealand's familiar settings are Blue Nile, The Spotted Cat, and Snug Harbor (all on Frenchmen Street), and Siberia and Cafe Istanbul on St. Claude. She arrived in New Orleans in 2005 with a degree in music composition from Oberlin Conservatory of Music and another from Jacques Lecoq's school of physical theatre in Paris. I have a handle on the former. A physical theatre in Paris offers up visions of Marcel Marceau and Jacques Tati having orchestrated pie fights while Jacques Brel plays in the background.

That's not so very far off from some of her appearances. She does at times perform with a gas mask and an accordion. Nealand, however, also has a more serious side, most notably when she plays soprano sax and clarinet at Preservation Hall with her traditional jazz band, The Royal Roses. Nealand sometimes performs with the Panorama Jazz Band, and she is also the singer in the rockabilly band, Rory Danger and the Danger Dangers. In addition, she is a member in Why Are We Building Such a Big Ship?, an amorphous group that consists of anywhere from six to ten members who play what's been called "half brass-band dirge and half indie-rock sea shanty." She is definitely one of the more interesting singers in New Orleans, but there's always this Yma Sumac sort of disconnect in her performances. Nealand clearly has loads of talent, but at times you'll wonder if she's just putting you on.

Mia Borders

Mia Borders started her professional music career in 2006, and she released eight new albums in just nine years. *USA Today* called her music "deeply funky." The *Times-Picayune* wrote, "She calls to mind Ani DiFranco, but funkier." Adding, she is a "singer-songwriter sui generis, playing sultry, often confessional original tunes sometimes cloaked in a thorny coat of high-energy, blues-rock riffage." So, we've established that she is funky and compellingly so.

Though she is based in New Orleans, Borders performs often at clubs and festivals elsewhere: Brazil's Bourbon Street Music Festival, Santa Cruz Blues Festival, Chattanooga's Nightfall Concert Series, Telluride Cajun Festival, Memphis's Levitt Shell, Wakarusa Music Festival, Long's Park Summer Music Series, and The Kennedy Center. Locally she'll be at New Orleans Jazz & Heritage Festival, Essence

Festival, House of Blues, and Tipitina's. She also appears at less-frequented spots like Ugly Dog Saloon, Richard Fiske's Martini Bar, and the New Orleans Public Library.

Ingrid Lucia

Ingrid Lucia didn't run away to the circus. Her family *was* the circus. She moved to New Orleans when she was 1 year old. Her father, going by the moniker Poppa Neutrino and his family, The Flying Neutrinos, spent 20 years as gypsies touring the world, living and traveling the United States and Europe in buses, tents, and amazing homemade rafts. The family became a band when Lucia was 11, and they played their self-taught Dixieland jazz on street corners, small halls, and anywhere anyone would listen. Her father was either a master showman or a first-class eccentric, depending on your orientation. When in New Orleans, he'd stand on Jackson Square, megaphone in one hand and a mannequin's leg in high heels as his musical instrument in the other.

Poppa Neutrino was also a huge classic movie buff. Lucia says in her RubyArts Agency profile, "I would grow up to be performing in a black and white movie." Instead, she would carry on the family business, keeping The Flying Neutrino's alive as the velvet-voiced front person. When I first heard her sing, I told my wife, "Close your eyes and you'll swear it's Billie Holiday." Since then, I've read this comparison by others seemingly a hundred times.

It has been Lucia's self-expressed desire to show a younger generation the power of traditional jazz and how it was the original rock and roll.

For whatever reason, she plays less often than many other live performers. These days she rarely takes the stage more than once a month. Nonetheless, you can catch her at a variety of venues: Three Muses, d.b.a. Rock 'n' Bowl, House of Blues, 30° × 90°, and The Bombay Club.

Meschiya Lake

Meschiya is the little girl who did run off to join the circus. Born in Oregon, she moved to South Dakota when she was 8 and literally joined the circus as a sideshow fire dancer and glass eater for the Know Nothing Family Zirkus Zideshow and The Circus at the End of the World. When the troupe took their off-season hiatus in New Orleans, Lake joined the long list of Ex-Pat-Y'ats (which includes me), or people who come to New Orleans for the first time, are immediately seduced, and decide that they have to live here. Said Lake in answering one of her 20 questions for Gonola. com, "I knew immediately that this was where I belonged. I am just so happy to live in a place where, if a guy rides by on a bike in full red body paint at 2:00 p.m. on a Monday, he isn't considered weird."

At first, Lake performed with The Loose Marbles and other street musicians on Royal Street. In 2009, she formed The Little Bighorns jazz band. They started out also playing in the streets, but then slowly started getting gigs in clubs. They are now one of the essential acts to see in New Orleans. I try to take all my out-of-town visitors to one of their performances, and I get to watch their jaws drop as they take in her sultry voice and the band's casual but completely tight jazz mastery. She has been awarded Best Female Vocalist the last four years, and counting.

I've described Lake as looking like she belongs painted on the front of a B-52 Bomber. She resembles a 1940s beauty queen, except for her many, many, many tattoos. The band plays regularly at d.b.a. and once or twice a week at The Spotted Cat. They have frequented Little Gem Saloon, and Lake performs without the band (but with premier pianist, Tom McDermott) on Wednesdays at Chickie Wah Wah.

Babs Evangelista

CHAPTER 9

Street Music

Apparently people have been playing music in the streets as long as there has been a city here. You go to other places and they try to create what we already have here—some cities pay people to create this cultural life!

—**Mary Howell**

Each day the section of Royal Street between St. Ann and St. Louis streets in the French Quarter is closed off from automobile traffic, essentially making it a pedestrian mall. During these hours, Royal Street will be lined with mimes, magicians, and people who pretend to be statues and get paid in quarters and dollars for literally doing nothing. The top draw, however, is always the street musicians. It's a tradition that goes back hundreds of years, of buskers mentoring younger generations and passing down an integral part of the city's culture.

A number of New Orleans's most noted musicians got their start on the street, including Troy "Trombone Shorty" Andrews, The Rebirth Brass Band, Dirty Dozen Brass Band, the lesser-known but beautifully named Emile "Stalebread" Locoume and his Razzy Dazzy Spasm Band, and Louis Armstrong. In his autobiography, Louis Armstrong describes his musical start: "We began by walking down Rampart Street between Perdido and Gravier. Singing at random we wandered through the streets until someone called to us to sing a few songs. Afterwards we would pass our hats and at the end of the night we would divvy up."

A young Henry Byrd found a discarded piano in the alley and began banging out tunes on French Quarter pavement. He would go on to become Professor Long-hair, the originator of the New Orleans sound that is a vivacious rumba-rhythmed piano blues. Meschiya Lake, named best female vocalist 2012–15, got her start singing for tips on Royal before becoming a regular at clubs like The Spotted Cat and Chickie Wah Wah, cutting three award-winning CDs, and touring internationally. Louis Michot, a member of the Grammy-nominated Lost Bayou Ramblers, said, "It was a huge part of my musical training. I learned how to connect my music with the people hearing it on the street. That's just so New Orleans."

Because of the transient nature of street performers, it's hard to pin down who will be playing where and when. Listed below are a few of the current regulars.

Tanya & Dorise are a popular duet most often performing on weekends on Royal at St. Louis Street. The violin-playing Tanya is thought to be the inspiration for the character Annie in HBO's *Treme*. Dorise plays the guitar, banjo, and a Casio keyboard strapped to her back. The duo even have a website (tanyandorise.com), where you can order any or all of their 10 CDs.

The bluesy-country husband-and-wife team known as David and Roselyn have been playing on the streets of the Quarter since 1975. They've recorded six albums and do performance tours on the West Coast and overseas. The couple has four grown children who they've put through school, paid for by performance tips earned on French Quarter streets.

Doreen Ketchens is an acclaimed clarinet player, husband Lawrence plays the tuba, trombone, and piano, and their daughter, Dorian, plays the drums. They play traditional New Orleans-style jazz most weekends in front of Rouses Market at Royal and St. Peter streets.

Trumpet player Kenny Terry founded a number of New Orleans brass bands, including Junior Olympia Brass Band and the New Birth Brass Band. He gathers a rotating assortment of first-rate musicians most days between 11:00 a.m. and 3:00 p.m. in front of The Cabildo.

The star and most photographed street performer is Grandpa Elliot. Looking like Uncle Remus, with his white beard, red shirt, straw hat, and overalls, the nearly blind singer and harmonica player can be found most days at Toulouse and Royal. He's also participated in Playing For Change, a project that recorded street musicians around the world, and has performed on *The Tonight Show* and *The Colbert Report*. His participation in "Stand By Me" has racked up more than 70 million hits on YouTube.

Decatur Street draws many of the "dirty kids," or transients who tend to smell worse and play worse than who you'll encounter on Royal Street or Jackson Square.

WWOZ's Reya Sunshine Hart and Charlie Steiner have produced a series of video "Busker Blogs," which provide an in-depth look at the city's street musicians. But, when we say "street music" in New Orleans, it means so much more than a couple of musicians and an upside-down hat or open instrument case to collect tips. There are entire traditions of second line, brass band, and Mardi Gras Indians that go back centuries.

Brass Bands

Brass bands go all the way back before there was a New Orleans, actually all the way back before there was brass, and the military bands were just drum and fife. The earlier name for fife was Schweizerpfeife, or Swiss flute. Okay, now I'm just showing off.

Beginning in the 16th century, armies adapted and trained drummers and fifers to provide signals to direct troops, give them the hour of the day, and sound alarms, as well as to play popular music as entertainment while on the march. Adolphe Sax, a Frenchman and namesake of the saxophone, was the most noted of several inventors who developed a family of chromatic-valved bugles. In America, horns overtook woodwinds as the principal instruments for bands. By 1835, the first all-brass bands were established.

Pre-brass brass bands have performed in New Orleans almost since the city's inception. French military records identified more than 100 French men in this city who performed in fife and drum bands prior to 1763. In 1838, the New Orleans *Picayune* reported that "a passion for horns and trumpets has reached a real mania." The two most popular brass bands in New Orleans in the 1850s were the Bothe's Brass Band and Charley Jaeger's Brass Band. Both bandleaders were European immigrants who came to New Orleans during the 1840s. Jaeger was from Alsace-Lorraine, France, and Bothe was from Hanover, Germany. Their bands played for parades, dances, and general entertainment.

Patrick Sarsfield Gilmore was born in Ireland, immigrated to this country, and became the father of brass band music in America. Gilmore became the leader of the prestigious Boston Brass Band. Then, during the Civil War, he was put in charge of organizing bands for the Union Army. He organized more than 300 bands for Union forces.

One of the brass bands, comprised of 32 African Americans, Gilmore brought from Boston to the then-occupied New Orleans in 1864. For two months, this band, identified in the press as Gilmore's Famous Band, performed almost on a daily basis. They marched down St. Charles Avenue and played in Jackson Square, Congo Square, and Lafayette Square. Not surprisingly, a tight, well-drilled, all African American band made quite the impression on the Creoles and blacks then living in New Orleans.

On January 26, 1864, they performed a "Promenade Concert" at the French Opera House. This was the first time that all races of people in New Orleans were invited to the same party. During this concert Gilmore premiered his composition "When Johnny Comes Marching Home Again." Two months later, for the inauguration of Governor Michael Hahn, Gilmore performed what was reservedly described in the press as "possibly the greatest musical event in the history of the world." Using civilians and brass band members, he assembled 500 musicians, a choir of 10,000 voices, a drum and bugle corps of 5,000, 50 cannons to be fired, and 4 regiments of infantry who accompanied the music by firing their rifles. He had all the public churches ring their bells upon his direction, which was accomplished by connecting them to a telegraph service from his podium on Lafayette Square. While there were no cell phones to record the event, word has it that the show was bigger than Led Zeppelin's reunion tour of 2007 or any Super Bowl halftime show.

Gilmore's Famous Band helped create the New Orleans style of brass bands. He did so by taking his European-styled military band music and stirring it (thoroughly) with the local sound, which itself was infused with African musical traditions. The earliest New Orleans–based bands include the Eureka Brass Band, the Onward Brass Band, the Excelsior Brass Band, the Tuxedo Brass Band, the Young Tuxedo Brass Band, and the Olympia Brass Band. The sound and style of these bands was worlds apart from the John Philip Souza stilted type of songs such as "You're a Grand Old Flag" that were being played in other parts of the country. Brass band here developed at the same time as the beginnings of jazz. Many jazz founders, including Kid Ory, Buddy Bolden, Sidney Bechet, and Louis Armstrong played in brass bands as well as their jazz bands.

Bunk Johnson was the first to record New Orleans–style brass band music (no, seriously) with his 1945 album, *New Orleans Parade*. His album was followed with records by the Eureka Brass Band in 1951 and the Young Tuxedo Brass Band in 1957.

The 1960s almost wiped out brass band music. Young musicians were getting into funk and viewed brass band as even moldier figs than doo-wop and Calypso. Pretty much one man, Danny Barker, saved brass band from fading into the dusty archives of history. He formed the Fairview Baptist Church Christian Marching Band. This decidedly uncool-sounding group kicked up the older brass band sound by making the "back row" (drums and tuba) much more prominent and integrating some hipper bebop stylings. The music was funkier and faster, and it led to a whole new renaissance that continues to this day. If you want to instantly hear the difference, bring up Eureka's classic "Didn't He Ramble" and sample it next to Rebirth Brass Band's contemporary classic "Do Whatcha Wanna."

There is no doubt you can hear live brass band this very evening. The To Be Continued Brass Band (that's their name) will probably be at their usual spot on Bourbon Street at Canal. The Young Fellaz Brass Band may be playing out on Frenchmen Street. Their unwillingness to tone it down in front of clubs that feature other performers, getting high, helping themselves to club food, and a generally lousy attitude has made them less than popular with Frenchmen Street shop and club owners, but their music draws a crowd. The Y&T (Young and Talented) brass band may be there on Frenchmen instead. They look young, about 13 years old, and they are indeed talented.

The top brass bands, all of which started out on the street, have largely locked up associations with bars and music clubs.

Rebirth Brass Band

Rebirth Brass Band, which won a Grammy Award in 2012, is quite simply New Orleans's best. I hope the Hot 8, Dirty Dozen, or the Soul Rebels are no more offended than Bill Russell, Oscar Robertson, or Magic Johnson would be for hearing Michael Jordan being called the best. They're all great.

Rebirth formed in 1983 by local legends the Frazier brothers, Keith and Phil, and Kermit Ruffins when they all still attended Clark High School in Tremé. Glen David Andrews and Corey Henry joined later.

SPOTLIGHT

Maple Leaf Bar

8316 Oak St.

Phone: 504-866-9359

Maple Leaf Bar (on Oak Street not Maple Street) is what a bar should be. The dented tin walls of the shotgun-shaped rooms are hung with old photographs of Mardi Gras queens from the '30s and '40s. The place is dark. It's most often packed with people ready to shake their booty. Your feet stick to the floor.

The bar has a rich history. It's loosely veiled as "The Raintree Street Bar," an Ellen Gilchrist's short story, has appeared in numerous poems (the Everette C. Maddox Memorial Prose & Poetry Reading, which is held there every Sunday, is the oldest poetry-reading series in North America), and has been used in movies. Much of *Angel Heart* with Mickey Rourke and Robert DeNiro was filmed at the bar.

Gifted musicians like Clifton Chenier and Buckwheat Zydeco often played at Maple Leaf Bar. Regulars today include Joe Krown (Sundays); Johnny Vidacovich (Thursdays); and the bar's signature event, the Rebirth Brass Band, plays (every Tuesday night).

Rebirth at the Maple Leaf has become a New Orleans tradition and is as iconic as any great musical event in the city. The band is billed to take the stage at 10:30 p.m. True to New Orleans style, where streetcars come when they come, I have never been there on a Tuesday night when the band started any earlier than 11:15 to 11:30. The late-night performance will be crowded, hot, and sweaty. The Rebirth will play so loud that your eardrums and nerves will be shaking for a few hours after the show has ended. In other words, a perfect night of live music.

They rejuvenated brass band by adding a little funk (and soul and hip hop and some Michael Jackson for good measure) to traditional arrangements. They've been changing and evolving the brass band sound ever since. There are those who feel their 2001 album release *Hot Venom* represents a turning point in brass band that is as dramatic as The Beatles's *Sgt. Pepper's Lonely Hearts Club Band* was to rock in 1967 or Miles Davis's *Kind of Blue* was to jazz in 1959. On the tracks of *Hot Venom*, the band collaborated with rappers Soulja Slim on "You Don't Want to Go to War" and Cheeky Blakk on "Pop That Pussy." They also incorporated hip hop with the streetwise song "Rockin' On Your Stinkin' Ass."

Members have likewise changed over the 30-year history of this band. Only the Frazier brothers remain from the original band. Phil Frazier is famous for his "elephant call" tuba blasts and Keith is renowned for powerful drumming.

I have seen Rebirth going on 10 times, and each time I listen in awe as their songs pretend to weave in and out of focus. Musicians seemingly cut loose from the band on high-energy improv and then, wham, they turn on a note and the group becomes the most unified and precise band you've ever heard.

Dirty Dozen Brass Band

Established in 1977, or four years before Rebirth, the Dirty Dozen Brass Band is largely credited with being the first to infuse brass band with bebop, R&B, and other more contemporary styles. Their efforts injected the music with an energy that attracted a younger audience. Using their freewheeling style, one of their songs even played off the TV theme song for *The Flintstones*. Trumpet player Gregory Davis, who, along with Roger Lewis on the baritone sax, has been with the band since the beginning and explained, "It's impossible to think that you can be exposed to the harmonies of Duke Ellington, the rhythms coming from Dizzy Gillespie, or the funk being done by James Brown, and then ignore it when you're playing New Orleans music."

The original band was largely made up of members of the defunct Hurricane Brass Band. Led by trumpeter Leroy Jones, ex-Hurricanes trumpeter Gregory Davis, sousaphonist Kirk Joseph, trombonist Charles Joseph, and saxophonist Kevin Harris, the band all continued to rehearse together. And they had a lot of time to rehearse because paying gigs had become rare when brass band was at an ebb.

The band has always tightrope-walked the line between honoring the roots of its traditions (when brass bands were primarily used for funeral dirges and jubilant second lines) and embracing the new street sound. In their current sets, you'll get a taste of old standards like "When the Saints Go Marching In" and brassy versions of today's hits like Rihanna's "Don't Stop the Music."

If you want a yabba-dabba-doo time tonight, you may be out of luck. Dirty Dozen has become primarily a large-venue festival band in New Orleans, and when on the road they play elegant music halls: places like the Granada Theater in Dallas, the Orpheum Theater in Flagstaff, and the Brooklyn Bowl in Las Vegas.

The Hot 8 Brass Band

The Hot 8 Brass Band holds court every Sunday night at Howlin' Wolf in the same way that Rebirth does its thing at the Maple Leaf on Tuesdays. Compared to Rebirth and the Dirty Dozen, Hot 8 came late to the party. Bennie Pete, Jerome Jones, and Harry Cook formed the band in 1995, merging two earlier bands: the Looney Tunes Brass Band and the High Steppers Brass Band. Their music equally blends hip hop, jazz, and funk styles with traditional New Orleans brass sounds.

The band is active in social causes. They brought music to shelters after Hurricane Katrina and started their own anti-violence campaign. Three of their members have been killed by gun violence: trumpet player Jacob Johnson, drummer Dinerral "Dick" Shavers, and trombone player Joseph "Shotgun Joe" Williams (who was shot by police).

Soul Rebels

If Sunday with the Hot 8 at Howlin' Wolf and Tuesday at the Maple Leaf with Rebirth have you hankering for another helping of brass band, then you need to check out the Soul Rebels who play every Thursday at Le Bon Temps Roule in Uptown.

Currently, they may be the most-traveled brass band. They are now playing more than 200 concerts a year all over the United States (they're regulars at the Bonnaroo Music Festival) and in Great Britain, South Africa, Brazil, and New Zealand. The Soul Rebels also have played with "everyone," from Green Day, Metallica, CeeLo Green, Galactic, Drive-By Truckers, Arcade Fire, Macklemore & Ryan Lewis, Rakim, Marilyn Manson, Slick Rick, Joey Badass, Pharoahe Monch, Robert Glasper, Black Thought (of The Roots), Prodigy (of Mobb Deep), Big Freedia, The String Cheese Incident, Styles P (of The Lox), Maceo Parker, Suzanne Vega, David A. Stewart (of the Eurythmics), Eric Krasno, Lettuce, Gov't Mule, John Medeski, and Juvenile.

The Village Voice website described them as "the missing link between Louis Armstrong and Public Enemy," though for me, I think there's more than one link between those particular artists.

Treme Brass Band

The Treme is the most traditional of the current brass bands. They are less interested in integrating funk, R&B, or Rhianna songs into their mix and are more focused upon what band leader, Benny Jones believes is essential. On NPR, he asserted that we "still need somebody to do the traditional music so we can pass that to the younger generation." Adding, "Somebody got to hold that spot down."

Their commitment to the old ways even includes a dress code. "Sound good, look good," says Jones. "My band always had the black pants, white shirts, ties, coats. That's a New Orleans tradition. What the older bands did years ago."

You can see them every Tuesday night at d.b.a. and Wednesdays at Candlelight Lounge.

Brass-A-Holics

Their name is really the Brass-A-Holics Go-Go Brass Funk Band, but for some reason no one ever calls them that. The band, formed in 2010 by trombonist Winston Turner, had the goal to merge the New Orleans brass sound with Washington, DC's go-go groove, a local sound with three standard congas and two junior congas.

They cover songs by Miles Davis, Nirvana, John Coltrane, Wham, Cyndi Lauper, Kanye West, and Louis Armstrong . . . all in one set.

The Original Pinettes Brass Band

The Original Pinettes might prefer you listen to them on the radio rather than see them live, because unless you're looking at them on stage you might never realize they are New Orleans's only all-female brass band. It took them years to be accepted as a first-rate band rather than a novelty act.

The band was created in 1991 by St. Mary's Academy school's band teacher Jeffrey Herbert. He chose 16 girls to create an all-female brass band. Percussionist Christie Jourdain, a sophomore at the time, was one of the 16 girls. More than two decades later, she is the only Original Pinettes Brass Band member remaining and is now the band's leader.

Stooges Brass Band

The Stooges was given their name from their audience, and it was inspired by the band's on-stage antics. Some of their off-stage behavior, however, has been less fun-filled. They may be best known for the fight they got into with Rebirth Brass Band at the Big Nine parade in 2009. I mean a fist-flying, tuba-denting fight, not just some name calling. Animosity between the two bands started back when the Stooges burst through the door of The Rock Bottom Lounge, horns blazing, during one of Rebirth's regular performances at the bar. I'm guessing that in their minds this was a way to challenge the established kings of New Orleans brass band. It's all rather odd because Rebirth was the inspiration for the Stooges—after seeing the Rebirth Brass Band play, Walter Ramsey went on to create his own band.

Since the Big Nine brawl, the Stooges have taken regular opportunities to call out Rebirth at second line parades and in social media. It feels kind of like the Cowboys versus Redskins rivalry in the NFL. (Although, to be a real rivalry it would help if the Redskins won now and again.)

But, unlike the Rebirth Brass Band, the Stooges have played in Hyderabad, India, as part of the U.S. Embassy–sponsored tour of India, Pakistan, Kyrgyzstan, and Tajikistan. I believe they are the only American band to ever play in Hyderabad, a pearl- and diamond-trading center in India. It would have been an act of karmic revenge had nagaras- and dhols-wielding Rajasthan musicians barged in to throw down with the Stooges.

The band plays and goofs around semi-regularly at d.b.a. and Blue Nile. They'll also be part of most festivals.

Second Line

Far more than playing at clubs and festivals, historically the most important function of New Orleans brass bands has been, and still is, to perform as second line parades at funerals.

Second line processions have been called the "quintessential New Orleans art form." The origins come from West Africa and the circle dance where adults formed the inner circle and children formed periphery circles. In the New Orleans style, the family of the deceased forms the first line. The second line are friends, more distant relatives, and people who didn't even know the corpse in life but want to join the party.

The first known African-American funeral that featured an African-American second line in New Orleans was in 1863 for Captain Andre Cailloux, who was killed during the Battle of Port Hudson. More than 10,000 African Americans turned out for his funeral.

Today, as in the days of yesteryear, brass bands accompany funeral parties from church to gravesite, playing traditional slow spiritual dirges and hymns like "Just a Closer Walk with Thee" and "Amazing Grace." Leaving the cemetery, however, it becomes a completely different tune. Handkerchiefs carried for sobbing and grief become a sashaying flag. Umbrellas used as protection from intense sun or rain become a festively twirling joystick. The music kicks way up to New Orleans style. "Some people call it funk," notes Big Chief Jake Millon in a 1976 documentary *The Black Indians of New Orleans*, "but to us it's strictly second line." Leaving the cemetery, the brass band begins what's been called "a jazz funeral without a body." Classic songs for the second line include "Hey Pocky A-Way," the 1960s Dixie Cups hit "Iko

Iko," and the newish (1990s) but seemingly timeless anthem of Rebirth Brass Band, "Do Whatcha Wanna."

Basically, a brass band-accompanied second line parade is a frenzied celebration for the life that was.

Mardi Gras Indians

Easily the most beautiful way New Orleanians take it to the streets is the tradition of Mardi Gras Indians. Mardi Gras Indians, a unique subculture exclusive to New Orleans, dates back to the 1700s. The most noteworthy (breathtaking) aspect is the costumes. Krewe members spend a year making intricately and intensely designed costumes that will be worn while parading for only one Mardi Gras and one St. Joseph's Day in March (well, some now also parade the Fairgrounds during Jazz Fest, which ends the first weekend in May). Then the labor-intensive costumes are ripped apart and krewe members start on new ones for the next year.

The elaborate costumes are a cross between the beading of West African rituals, brought here by the slaves, and the feathers of the Native American outfits. Both cultures share a reverence for the spirits of their ancestors and hold a strong belief in celebrations using ritual costumes. It was also a West African tradition to signal respect for one's hosts by dressing like them in ritual celebrations. Most books

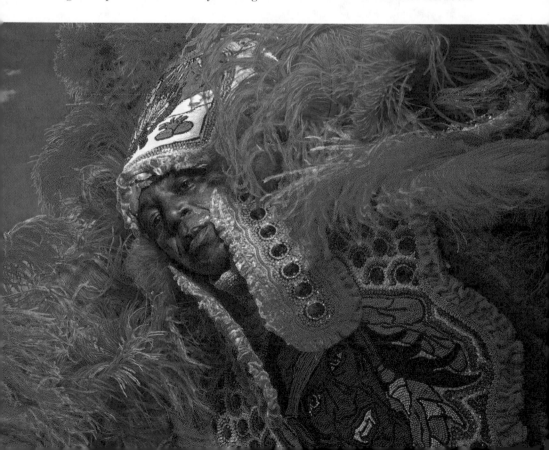

and wiki-statements-of-fact-like-things share a commonly held belief that escaped slaves first created these outfits to honor the Native Americans who took them in or otherwise assisted them after they ran away. Secret societies of masked warriors are also common to both African and Native American cultures.

Historically, blacks were not welcomed to participate in Mardi Gras. So the black neighborhoods in New Orleans developed their own style of celebrating. Rather than Rex, Bacchus, and Proteus, their krewes took on names of imaginary Indian tribes like Wild Magnolias, the Golden Star Hunters, Mohawks, Black Eagles, Wild Tchoupitoulas, Golden Blades, Little Red White & Blues, Wild Squatoolies, and Fi Yi Yi.

On Mardi Gras each year, "tribes" of black Indians parade through their own neighborhoods singing and dancing to traditional chants. In the past, this was a violent day for many Mardi Gras Indians. It was a day used to settle scores. The Big Chiefs of two different tribes would cross paths and start with chants, then ceremonial dances, and threatening challenges to "Humba," or a Big Chief's demand that the other Chief bow and pay respect. Often these confrontations would get violent.

Those practices changed, due largely to the leadership of Big Chief Allison "Tootie" Montana of the Yellow Pocahontas tribe. He redirected the confrontations so that they were not about knives or guns. They became more of an "I'm prettier than you!" *Project Runway* meets the *Slam Dunk* contest. The krewes with the best outfits were hailed the mightiest.

The culture has survived despite being forced underground twice, first banned by fearful whites after the 1811 Slave Revolt, and later when Jim Crow laws were put into effect in the 1890s.

Music has always been a vital part of the Mardi Gras Indian experience. The tradition of their music is a distinctive call-and-response vocals that is heavy with drums and tambourine. Songs like "Iko Iko," "Hey Pocky A-Way," and "Indian Red" have been used as standards by all tribes and covered by various artists such as The Meters, the Neville Brothers, Professor Longhair, Dr. John, the Dixie Cups, and yes, the Grateful Dead.

If somehow you've reached this point in your life without knowing Mardi Gras Indian music, I suggest you bring up "Handa Wanda" on a device of your choice. I don't need to challenge you, wager a bet, or throw down a Humba. I already know I've won and that you are dancing yo ass off.

In the mid-1950s, folklorist Samuel Charters collected field recordings of Indians in New Orleans and released them on the Smithsonian Folkways label. Since then, the Wild Magnolias, Golden Eagles, Wild Tchoupitoulas, Bayou Renegades, Flaming Arrows, Guardians of the Flame, Wild Mohicans, and others have left the streets long enough to be recorded in the studio. A small handful may very well be performing in a club, dressed in full beaded and feathered gear, while you're here.

Wild Magnolias

The Wild Magnolias were among the very first tribes to perform their music publicly. In 1970, they recorded the revolutionary single, "Handa Wanda," and in 1974 they cut a full album. Since then they have been the highest profile group. For many years they were headed by Big Chief Bo Dollis, who passed away in January 2014. Their beyond funky tunes feature an eclectic range of instruments that include beer bottles, cans, snare drums, cymbals, and Big Chief's stunning vocals.

They've performed for President Clinton, for the Queen of England, at Carnegie Hall, and at the Rock and Roll Hall of Fame. The Wild Magnolias may well be playing tonight in New Orleans. Check Tipitina's calendar.

Big Chief Monk Boudreaux

Following the death of Bo Dollis, Big Chief Monk Boudreaux inherited the mantle as the biggest of the Big Chiefs. Boudreaux, a childhood friend of Bo Dollis, was with the Wild Magnolias for more than 30 years. After leaving in 2001, he's performed with the Golden Eagles as well as with famed New Orleans acts Anders Osborne, Galactic, and Papa Mali.

Today, he is one of the most well-known Mardi Gras Indians playing on an international stage. He remains committed to keeping the 200-year-old tradition alive. When an accompanying musician once asked him, "Hey Monk, what key is this song in?" he replied, "Boy, this goes back to before they even had keys!"

When not on the road, Big Chief Monk Boudreaux appears at Maple Leaf Bar and d.b.a.

CHAPTER 10

Musta Been the Wrong Place *at the* Wrong Time

(Rock & Roll and Punk)

Rock and roll is the hamburger that ate the world. —**Peter York**

Fred LeBlanc of Cowboy Mouth has said of the New Orleans music scene, "Rock is sort of treated like the red-headed stepchild." That's probably overstating the case a bit, but in a city renowned for jazz, blues, R&B, and funk, rock 'n' roll does take second fiddle. There's been no noteworthy movement like grunge rock in Seattle, glam rock in New York, or garage bands of Detroit and Cleveland.

Well, there was a brief New Orleans movement called sludge metal in the early '90s, but I sense this is the first you've heard of it. Groups like Crowbar, Acid Bath, and Eyehategod created a dark and gloomy sound. If you YouTube Crowbar's "hit" song, "Existence Is Punishment," you'll get a sense of sludge from this four-minute video (unless you decide to kill yourself halfway through). Guitarist, lead vocalist, and founder Kirk Windstein continually reassembles members of Crowbar to keep the band going. They released their 10th album, *Symmetry in Black*, in 2014.

One of the first New Orleans rock groups to get any national attention was Zebra, founded in 1975. The group featured Randy Jackson on guitar and vocals. No, not the Randy "Yo! Check it out, dawg. I'm just keepin' it real" Jackson, the cliché-spinning former judge on *American Idol*. Originally a cover band of Led Zeppelin, The Moody Blues, and Rush songs, Zebra started doing original material and gaining modest fame in the '80s, only to shut it down in 1993 when Randy formed his own New York–based band, Randy Jackson's China Rain.

Prior to the '70s there were rock bands in New Orleans that at least garnered local attention. Mention bands like Noah's Wax Battleship, Paper Steamboat, or Moon Dawgs and the Gaunga Dyns to any New Orleanian over the age of 50 and you're likely to get a smile of recognition.

Just in the way you may occasionally need a cheeseburger between Cajun and Creole meals, there are a handful of rock groups that might provide you with a needed break from our jazz and blues.

Cowboy Mouth

Cowboy Mouth (along with Better Than Ezra) are the two current bands most known to people not from New Orleans, and most revered by rock fans who live in New Orleans. Cowboy Mouth has been around since the early '90s, has released a dozen records, and has been featured on TV and radio stations nationwide. They are best known as a high-volume, powerhouse live act. Their performances have been likened to "a religious experience." Said frontman Fred LeBlanc, "If the Neville Brothers and The Clash had a baby, it would be Cowboy Mouth." They've cut back from being constantly on the road and now do about 50 live performances a

year. In the New Orleans area, they can fill the Smoothie King Center, the same venue where the NBA Pelicans play. If you're lucky you might catch them for free during the Lafayette Square series. They play festivals and were Tulane University's 2015 Homecoming dance band, which makes them seem less cool than they are.

Better Than Ezra

Better Than Ezra recorded a lot of indie releases on their own label, Swell Records, before being signed by Elektra. Their very first demo cassette tape, circulated in 1988, is supposedly worth bejillions (well . . . a lot). Their single, "Good," from their first Elektra release reached #1 on the Hot Modern Rock Tracks chart and the album went platinum. Band member Tom Drummond commented on CNN: "It took us seven years to get signed, and then seven weeks to get to number one."

Anders Osborne

Anders Osborne's music is sometimes considered blues. He's written country hits for Tim McGraw and has toured with a band featuring the Mardi Gras Indians' Big Chief Monk Boudreaux. But to me he is mostly a classic rock 'n' roll singer strapped with a guitar and a New Orleans take on Neil Young or Jackson Browne.

He's also the embodiment of the great Miles Davis quote "It takes a long time to be able to play like yourself." Anders left his homeland of Sweden when he was 16, then experienced a lifetime and a half in America battling bipolar disorder and various addictions to anything you can drink, shoot, or snort. He describes those

years in a *Gambit Weekly* newspaper interview: "All the terrible stories that come with addiction, I have them. Blacking out, waking up not knowing where my guitar is, and I've been running around with no pants on for two days."

Osborne finally settled down both figuratively and literally in his adopted hometown of New Orleans. "New Orleans clicked for me. It's not something I have to reach for or touch. I am this city. I am becoming it, making it, shaping it. You have to constantly work on New Orleans, be a part of it. Carry on traditions while you make new ones."

His output (13 albums) and his range (from acoustic singer-songwriter to ferocious electric guitar-hero) is impressive. He's won *OffBeat Magazine*'s "Best Songwriter" the past two years, and he has been "Best Guitarist" three years and counting. If Osborne had only written just the one song "Summertime in New Orleans" and then quit, he'd still have a locked-up place on my Forever list.

The Generationals

Another group worth your time and attention is the Generationals, a two-person band consisting of Ted Joyner and Grant Widmer. They were previously a five-member band, The Eames Era, possibly best known for the song "Could Be Anything" that was featured on the TV show *Grey's Anatomy*. When three of the five quit, Ted and Grant became a New Orleans version of two-person bands like the White Stripes or the Black Keys.

Grant Widmer says of their New Orleans roots: "My reality of being from New Orleans was growing up and watching MTV. I grew up in Lakeview and there wasn't a second line going down the street. Beavis and Butthead was probably the most formative thing."

Caddywhompus

Caddywhompus is our other White Stripes or Black Keys, again consisting of only two members, but they blast a wall of sound of a much larger band. Sean Hart's polyrhythmic drumming and Chris Rehm's untrained or at least undertrained vocals and guitar have been crafting abstract pop tunes since they were classmates in middle school. The word *caddywhompus* is a colloquialism meaning "crooked" or "uneven." Whether that's a good thing or a bad thing depends on your taste.

The Revivalists

The Revivalists seem like a huge band in comparison with the previous two, given it has seven members (sometimes more when they add in an oh-so-New Orleans brass section). They blast out a sound that *Rolling Stone* magazine described as "a Crescent City–rhythm spin on jam-band jubilee." The band got their start when guitarist Zack Feinberg and drummer Andrew Campanelli first met during jam sessions at Tipitina's Sunday Music Workshops. The two then found their frontman, guitarist and singer David Shaw, by pure luck when they rode past Shaw singing on his front porch. The then-newly formed Revivalists got their first live performance shot at the dive bar/laundromat Checkpoint Charlie's during an open mic audition.

Hurray for the Riff Raff

Wilco bills themselves as alternative rock. Lucinda Williams has been called American rock, folk, blues, and country. New Orleans band Hurray for the Riff Raff mines a similar vein. The band's fiddler, Yosi Perlstein, describes their music: "I think our sound is pretty unique. The band is influenced by a lot of different styles. You can hear influences from Appalachian old time, old R&B, and gospel to '60s rock and roll with some New Orleans and Cajun sounds. You just have to listen to it for it to make sense."

It's not really a traditional New Orleans sound, though the songs are layered with New Orleanian lyrics. Singer-songwriter and banjo-guitar player Alynda Lee Segarra is the face of Riff Raff. She grew up in the Bronx and is of Puerto Rican

Ryan Hodgson-Rigsbee

descent. Growing up, she was a regular at the hardcore punk shows at ABC No Rio in NYC. At age 17 she pulled a Woody Guthrie, left home, and crossed America hopping freight trains. Like so many artists, writers, and musicians, when she arrived in New Orleans, the city gave her that vortex feeling of "home." She's said to *OffBeat,* "Living here, it's really great because a lot of musicians are not playing to become famous or succeed in a monetary way, but because they love to play."

Since settling in New Orleans, Segarra (who is only 26 as I write this) and her band have already made six albums, and have been chosen Emerging Artist of the Year. Their 2014 album, *Small Town Heroes,* was named as one of the best albums of the year by *Rolling Stone* and *Spin* magazines, and NPR.

Hurray for the Riff Raff is in the "intense road trips" stage of their career. But when they're in town they can be heard at One Eyed Jacks, House of Blues, and at every Jazz Fest.

Sun Hotel

Sun Hotel is an Indie band with a capital "I" that sometimes sounds like Brian Eno ambient music and other times like a straight-up rock and roll band. Don't hold the things written about them by other people as a reason not to give them even a sampling. When I read that Sun Hotel is "the most earnest quintessence of the uncompromisingly guarded yet wholly collaborative nature of songwriting, in an era over-congested with charlatanistic pseudo-artists, by applying a punk ethic to the familiar sounds of post-gospel, suffusing every guitar string, bass rattle and whisper with wave after wave of echo-imbued reverb, in-house living room recording prodigy manages to balance the pop leanings of the album's infectious hooks with deafening walls of white noise while the concussive rhythms of their multi-percussion setup create a chaotic rumble throughout," I considered sprinting to find the simple nonsense of my old bubble gum Monkees and Herman's Hermits albums—just to shake out the idea of whatever "post-gospel" might be from the chaotic rumble in my head.

Phil Anselmo

Phil Anselmo is sort of the New Orleans renaissance man of punk rock. He is best known as the former lead singer of Pantera, but he has had many start-up and side project bands such as Eibon, a very short-lived supergroup; Southern Isolation, which recorded just four songs before breaking up; Superjoint Ritual; Philip H. Anselmo & the Illegals; and Christ Inversion, a short-lived metal project where Anselmo played guitar under the name "Anton Crowley" and their lyrics were based on horror films and Satanism. The group Down has been Anselmo's main recording and touring band since 2006.

Anselmo also started his own record label in 2001, Housecore Records, and is involved in a YouTube comedy series called *Metal Grasshopper*, with comedian Dave Hill. In addition, he was the founder of one of the country's most highly regarded Halloween attractions, House of Shock. Anselmo owns an extensive collection of several thousand horror films and possesses a world-class knowledge of horror films that would rival the late great Forrest J. Ackerman.

Rik Slave

I could go on and annotate any number of bands from Bipolaroid, Clockwork Elvis, Sick Like Sinatra, and Buck Biloxi and the Fucks if only for the joy of typing their names, but we have other musicians to cover. I will, however, mention Rik Slave here primarily because he's a friend and he works by day at one of my favorite food stops, Cochon Butcher. But I'm also mentioning him here because he's been called "one of rock's best kept secrets, and one of its great performers" by the online music guide AllMusic.

Chet Overall

Rail thin, with a greased back receding hairline and a pencil-thin John Waters mustache, I have more than once said that Slave looks like a late-night TV horror host. As a singer since 1986, he has fronted a wide range of bands from sludge rock or punk bands like Swamp Goblin and the Cretinous to a brief fling with a hard-edged punk band, Man Scouts of America, to a truly bent country band, Rik Slave & the Phantoms, to his newer, benter country band, Rik Slave's Country Persuasion (Slave has said, "Every punk rocker goes through a Hank Williams phase") to the Ramones or Misfits vibe of his group Rock City Morgue and to a pure rock band The Cons and Prose.

It look Slave 20 years of performing before he recorded his first album. He admitted, "We don't like to rush into things."

Mike Shane

Discordant
(and Some of Our Best) Notes

I'm not sure, but I'm almost positive, all music came from New Orleans.
—Ernie K-Doe

Discordant music often means dissonant, harsh, or jarring sounds. And certain New Orleans musicians like Guglielmo fit that billing. Dressed as a clown, he sings opera arias while displaying magnificent feats of strength and endurance, including getting tattoos burned into his flesh while he performs. Guglielmo can sometimes be absorbed (much more than merely seen or heard) as the brunch entertainment at Live Oak Cafe or as part of Cirque du Gras, an offbeat circus collective.

But discordant can also mean "at variance" or "divergent." This chapter is meant to highlight the latter; skilled musicians who don't fit into a category or style of music.

Helen Gillet

Betraying my personal and unjustifiable taste, Helen Gillet is my #1 favorite Queen of Discordant Music in New Orleans. She plays the cello. She plays the cello in ways you've never heard it played, or even imagined it could be played.

Helen Gillet joined the New Orleans music scene in 2002 by way of Wisconsin, Chicago, Singapore, and the French-speaking section of Belgium (Wallonia), where she was born. She has a master's degree in classical music, but her training as an improvisor began with North Indian Hindustani vocal ragas, which are your basic old run-of-the-mill, heard-it-a-thousand-times Vedic ritual chants.

A session with Gillet will include French chansons, a sort of traditional French folk music from the 1930s to '50s, jazz, funk, rock, what she playfully calls Hungarian rock opera, and, my favorite, the songs she performs with live tape looping. Her masterful skill with looping is no mere gimmick, but is absolutely mesmerizing and

Helen Gillet   Michael Lancaster

trance inducing. For me, it's also a tear-jerking experience: It moves me to watch a real artist who is not the least bit focused on becoming a brand or with performing in a style that has a prayer of being packaged for radio air time.

Her wide range of talent has allowed her to play with Kid Koala, Smokey Robinson, Nikki Glaspie (who's played with Beyoncé, Dumpstafunk, and the Neville Brothers), John Popper (Blues Traveler), members of Morphine, Ani DiFranco, The New Orleans Klezmer All-Stars, The Mardi Gras Indian Orchestra, and a host of European avant-garde jazz musicians: Georg Graewe, Kresten Osgood, Tobias Delius, Frank Gratkowski, Almut Kuehne, and Wilbert de Joode. If you see a pattern here, please give me a call.

In New Orleans, Gillet can be heard at Antieau Gallery and the Blue Nile (upstairs). She plays every Monday night at Bacchanal, although the times I've seen her there have frustrated me: As backyard diners clink glasses, rattle plates, and talk too loudly they hardly notice that a true artist is performing right in front of their pairing of Jade Jagger wine and bacon-wrapped dates.

The New Orleans Bingo! Show

The New Orleans Bingo! Show is also my #1 favorite. (Dis & Dem, a great burger joint in Mid-City, has "The Only Omelette" on their menu, and just below, "The Only Other Omelette." So, I can have two #1 favorites.) The Bingo! Show is hard to define even after you've seen it. I have, in the past, described it as sort of a New Orleans hard-edged, slightly deviant version of Cirque du Soleil. Sideshows of original short films, comedic skits, and burlesque, featuring Miss Trixie Minx, serve as the framing device for the uber-talented Clint Maedgen (who also plays with the Preservation Hall Band) and his randy, eccentric, and costumed band.

The Bingo! Show started in 2002 when Maedgen found bingo game boards in a thrift store and was inspired to create the first version of the group that merged theater, rock, and a game of bingo. They at first played in the back room of Fiorella's

Cafe, but have progressed to become a semi-every-so-often performance at One Eyed Jacks. They've also played at the Kennedy Center.

I can't recommend strongly enough viewing Maedgen's YouTube video, "Complicated Life." For me, it captures the essence of New Orleans in five minutes and seven seconds.

Until he recently retired, the diminutive Ron Rona, in face paint, bowler hat, and megaphone, served as the emcee. After seeing the Bingo! Show a few times, I knew my then-10-year-old daughter would be captivated. I texted Ron to see if there were venues or occasions where the show was less packed with his mega-yelling "Mother Fuckers." There were. I took her to the Bingo! Show's outdoor performance during the French Quarter Festival. She was, indeed, captivated.

Their music runs the gambit, from a Nick Cave & The Bad Seeds sound all the way to the work of Kurt Weill. Some songs include the theremin. The theremin is an electronic musical instrument controlled by a performer waving their hands between two metal antennas. At no point does the musician actually touch the instrument. The eerie sound can be heard in many science fiction movies of the 1950s (think *The Day the Earth Stood Still* . . . the good one with Michael Rennie and Patricia Neal).

The Bingo Show   Mike Shane

Warning: The Bingo! Show stops in the middle of the performance to play bingo. If you win, for God's sake don't tell them . . . unless you want to be brought up on stage to experience the hilarity of utter humiliation.

Morella and the Wheels of If

Morella and the Wheels of If is the beautifully named duo, sometimes trio, and on rare occasions quartet that's something of a Bingo! Show mini-me. Brother and sister, Eric Laws, the pianist/composer/singer, and Laura Laws, writer/singer, perform what they call "Old-World Music for a Modern Time." They are known for their unique cabaret-style theatrical stage shows that incorporate videos and costumes. At times they are accompanied by guest musicians playing bass, drums, guitar, or violin. They play at Circle Bar, sometimes at d.b.a., many Sundays at Yuki Izakaya, and an assortment of parlors and art galleries.

Sweet Crude

If I had a #1B favorite discordant musician or group, it would be Sweet Crude. I "discovered" Sweet Crude after they'd been around two years, when they were the opening band for the group I went to see one night, the Wild Magnolias.

Sweet Crude, a seven-piece ensemble Cajun indie-rock group, could have been placed in the Rock & Roll and Punk chapter, or in the chapter about Cajun and zydeco music. I chose to place them here because (A) those chapters were long enough, and, more important, (B) Sweet Crude is neither fish nor foul. They're not really a Cajun band because they play with a percussion-heavy rock sensibility. And they're a pretty weird rock band because of their insistence on lyrics that are mostly Cajun French and their assembly of instruments, which is random and weird and quite wonderful. Most notably, they do without any lead guitars.

Percussionist Marion Tortorich described the process of how they put the band together in an *OffBeat Magazine* article, saying that members were chosen for the kind of energy they brought and "then we figured out what instruments they could play on different songs." What Sweet Crude ultimately put together was Alexis Marceaux and Sam Craft as vocalists (both of whom also drum, and Sam also plays violin), Tortorich and John Arceneaux as percussionists, keyboardists Skyler Stroup (who also plays trumpet) and Sam's brother Jack Craft, plus Stephen MacDonald on bass.

They also look discordant from what you might expect. While I'm certain band members are in their 20s, they look more like high school Mathletes or members of the camera club.

Debauche

Debauche, like Sweet Crude, could have been included in the rock 'n' roll chapter. However, the fact that they sing in Russian and call themselves a "Russian Mafia Band" slides them over to placement here. The group got its start as a one-man whacking crew in 2008. Ukrainian-born Yegor Romantsov sang what he called Russian hooligan songs at Kahve Royale coffee shop on Royal Street every Friday from 10:00 p.m. until midnight. He drank his homemade honey pepper vodka while singing. Gradually, like-minded performers found Yegor and wild Russian jam sessions soon began breaking out. I sense only in New Orleans would there have been like-minded performers. Eve Venema and Christian Kuffner of the former Zydepunks joined in. Then violinist Jesse Stoltzfus broke his hand and couldn't play, so he started with the band as a drummer. Now he's mastered both instruments and can play drums and violin simultaneously. He can also ride a unicycle and juggle at the same time. More ex-Zydepunks, bass player Scott Potts and drummer Joseph McGinty joined in. Vincent Schmidt, an accordion player from an Oregon Russian

Roman Alokhin

by Roman Alokhin

band, Chervona, was game. Kerry Lynn, a belly-dancing percussionist, is the latest addition. Their sound is similar to Gogol Bordello and the Leningrad band style, which were made popular by the 2005 movie, *Everything Is Illuminated.*

Tank and the Bangas

Terriona "Tank" Ball sounds like she's campaigned to be included in the Discordant section when she stated that "They (New Orleanians) have never experienced anything like this before. And vice versa." Named "Tank" by her father (gee, thanks Dad), Bell began her career as a spoken word poet. And she pretty much still is, though now she's backed up by singers Angelika Joseph and Kayla Jasmine, and a first-rate seven-piece band. In her sweet pixie voice she creates and delivers some of the most oddly wonderful lyrics about the most wonderfully odd subject matter.

In one song she compares shopping at Whole Foods versus Winn-Dixie as a metaphor of lost love. Walmart figures in another song as a place to shop for the perfect mate where you can check the tag on their collar to see if they had any issues you might have to deal with later. Leaving her retail store comfort zone, one of the Bangas "hits?" is a song called "Bradys." It's about her longing for the comfortingly plastic lifestyle of Florence Henderson on the famed '60s TV show *The Brady Bunch.*

Quintron

To many in New Orleans, Quintron is the unquestionable #1 discordant hero. It's hard to imagine a performer more at odds with every other musician or musical style. Since 1994 he's been cutting records, 14 albums in all, inventing strange musical contraptions, and entertaining audiences with a combination of psychedelic soul live music performances and inflatable puppet theater put on by his wife, Miss Pussycat. I'm just getting started. But underneath all the weird electronics and puppetry, Quintron does manage to pull off a very danceable B-52's sound.

Quintron has released strange soundscape recordings based on taping inner-city frogs and neighborhood ambience. He has also holed himself up in the New Orleans Museum of Art (for three months) to create the epic album, *Sucre Du Sauvage.*

His inventions include the Spit Machine, a hand organ that uses saliva as a tuning conductor and the Disco Light Machine, a device attached to a drum kit that lights up to accompany the beat. The harder you play the drums, the brighter the light and the louder the electronic sounds. His most significant invention, however, is the Drum Buddy. It is a light-activated analog synthesizer that creates murky, low-fidelity, rhythmic patterns. The Drum Buddy has been used by Wilco and Laurie Anderson.

Quintron used to play regular shows at Spellcasters Lodge, which Quintron owned in the Bywater neighborhood. Their own Facebook page currently states that Spellcasters "may be permanently closed." As of this writing, Quintron has upcoming shows confirmed at One Eyed Jacks and Gasa Gasa.

Cole Williams

Brooklyn-bred Cole Williams recently moved to New Orleans (January 2015) and has rapidly become one of the new "wow" performers. She's a composer, producer, entrepreneur, WWOZ radio host, grade school music teacher with her own jewelry line, and, above all else, a powerful singer.

Cole performs at the Maple Leaf and Chickie Wah Wah with her band, That's Our Cole. Her gender-bending music has been termed "African rock meets Jamaican soul," but perhaps it is best described by the title of her album, *Out of the Basement, Out of the Box.*

DJ Soul Sister

DJ Soul Sister is not a live musician, but a revered DJ who puts on an intensely lively spin of Motown, old R&B, and techno-pop every Saturday night at the Hi-Ho Lounge. The show runs 11:00 p.m. to 3:00 a.m.

Known as the "queen of rare groove," DJ Soul Sister has hosted her "Soul Power" show on WWOZ radio for nearly two decades. Soul Sister has created her seamlessly blended, vinyl-only sets everywhere from New York to Los Angeles to London. Here in New Orleans, DJ Soul Sister's dance parties are regarded and respected and attended as much as any live jazz, blues, rock, R&B, and funk show.

SPOTLIGHT

Dive Bar Alley

There's a stretch of bars and clubs along St. Claude Avenue from the Marigny to Bywater that is much less frequented than Frenchmen Street. But it offers far more eclectic music, burlesque, and some performances that must be experienced because they can't be described.

AllWays Lounge

2240 St. Claude Ave.
Phone: 504-218-5778

You never know what you'll find at the AllWays Lounge until you walk in the door. Well, I guess you could look at their calendar online. When Nancy, my favrette cuzzane (yes, we call each other that), was visiting New Orleans, our bar hopping included the AllWays. That night it was amateur striptease night. Trust me, you don't want to see amateur striptease. We quickly left and went across the street to The Hi-Ho Lounge. There, it was bounce night. A significantly overweight white guy was doing some pretty amazing things with his gelatinous buttocks, where each cheek gyrated as if responding to completely different neurons.

On other nights, however, the AllWays is exactly where you want to be.

The club has weekly readings where the series name, Esoterica, gives away their twist. They also host the Freaksheaux to Geaux, a professional burlesque variety act, and regular shows by Bella Blue ("Pussy Magic") and Dirty Dime Peep Show. Thursdays are drag bingo with Vinsantos. Musically, the AllWays (not surprisingly) leans toward alternative music, head banging rock, and the unclassifiable weirdness of acts like Ratty Scurvics. Sunday's the AllWays provides free swing music dance lessons.

Kajuns Pub

2256 St. Claude Ave.
Phone: 504-947-3735

What you'll hear at Kajuns may not fit your definition of music. It is the top karaoke bar in town, every night starting at 9:00 p.m. A wide range of songs to ravage are offered, including tunes from Pee-wee Herman films. During the football season, Kajuns gives out free jello shots every time the Saints score a touchdown. Lately, that's not been often enough.

The Saturn Bar

3067 St. Claude Avenue
Phone:

The Saturn was voted Best Dive Bar in America five times (yes, there is such an award). On the outside, the graffiti-covered plank boards on the windows make it look like a place you shouldn't enter. However, crack open the door and it's like Dorothy landed in Oz. You'll be greeted by technicolor, bizarre paintings and light fixtures overhead, ratty booths, and six jukeboxes (none of them work).

The funk is every night, but live music is a sometimes thing. Regulars performers like Alex McMurray, Elisa Ambrosia, Rotary Downs (none of them otherwise in this book) will draw . . . well, not exactly crowds, but someone to talk to. Larger crowds actually show up for dance nights, such as the once-a-month Mod Night.

Siberia
2227 St. Claude Ave.
Phone: 504-265-8855

Siberia books punk, metal, bounce, and . . . it may be the only place in town where you can hear Slavic music. Plus there's weekly burlesque and some of the worst comics you'll ever hear. At the back of the bar, past the taxidermied deer and turkeys, is a pop-up restaurant, Kukhnya ("kitchen" in Russian), that serves Slavic soul food, pierogi, blini, and kielbasa. This bar recently edged out the legendary Tipitina's as the people's choice award for number one live music club.

The Hi-Ho Lounge
2239 St. Claude Ave.
Phone: 504-945-4446

The Hi-Ho Lounge has live music most nights that ranges to everything from hip hop and funk to indie rock. Their best night is Saturday when DJ Soul Sister hosts her Hustle Dance Party (11:00 p.m. to

3:00 a.m.), spinning a lively mix of R&B classics, Motown, and techno pop. One night I was there, the Detroit Party Marching Band (sort of Detroit's version of the Hungry March Band) chose to have half their band jump up on the bar itself to play. No one objected.

In addition to live music, the Hi-Ho hosts premier burlesque groups including Rev. Spooky LeStrange and Her Billion Dollar Baby Dolls, Storyville Starlettes, and Slow Burn Burlesque.

Sweet Lorraine's Jazz Club
1931 St. Claude Ave.
Phone: 504-945-9654

Sweet Lorraine's is the closest to the French Quarter of the clubs on Dive Bar Alley. Unlike most of the others, Sweet Lorraine's never has burlesque nor cringe-inducing comedians. Sweet Lorraine's is instead focused solely on outstanding blues and jazz with the occasional spoken word and jazz poetry session. The live jazz Sunday brunch is more locals/less touristy than the more famous Commander's Palace, Crystal Room, or Court of Two Sisters.

CHAPTER 12

Gangsta Gumbo—
Hip Hop, Rap, and Bounce

All I can do is do what I do and make it do what it does. —Big Freedia

While writing about voodoo in my book *Fear Dat,* my wife warned me not to mess around with my often irreverent (some might say snarky) attitude. We didn't want bad juju visited upon us. I needed no such warning here. New Orleans rap artist, B. G. a.k.a. Baby Gangsta a.k.a. Christopher Dorsey is serving 14 years in a federal prison for gun possession and witness tampering. I think I'll play this chapter more or less straight. Na mean?

Unlike rock 'n' roll and punk, where New Orleans is more of a tag along, the city played an important role in the development of hip hop and rap, and provided the foundation of bounce music. However, locally these styles are still relegated to maybe one act (usually Juvenile or Lil Wayne) of the hundreds on the stages at the Jazz & Heritage Festival, and maybe one or two articles a year in local print, including *OffBeat,* a monthly magazine completely devoted to local music. After Hurricane Katrina, there were many concerts performed nationwide and CD collections released as tributes to honor and preserve the essential music of New Orleans: jazz, blues, second line, and our rumba-boogie-funk. There were no such concerts or collections to celebrate our rich rap or bounce scene.

You'll note that I'm guilty as well, shoving my Gangsta Gumbo chapter at the back of this book. It would appear that I too assume this chapter may not be of high interest to the majority of my readers. Nonetheless, I'll try to cover the main players and stories of our hip hop, rap, and bounce music scene. Unfortunately, I do not have the room to detail the work of Henry "Palomino" Alexander, Ice Mike, DJ Captain Charles, Raj Smooth (called the greatest DJ in the world), Bust Down, Kilo, Mobo Joe, Devious, Gregory D, nor tens if not hundreds of others who form a core part of this music scene.

Southern rap or hip hop, also called Dirty South, emerged in the 1980s as a reaction against the belief that New York City and Los Angeles could be the only legitimate homes for the music. Just by virtue of not being from LA or New York, many artists were marginalized, and so had a hard time getting record contracts.

By the '90s, Southern rap started to emerge. Noteworthy artists and new and significant labels earned a place of prominence. We can look to three cities in particular: Miami, with 2 Live Crew and "booty rap"; Atlanta with its bass-heavy party rap performers Arrested Development and OutKast; and New Orleans with its commercial enterprises, most notably the labels No Limit Records and Cash Money.

Master P built a rap empire with No Limit Records. Originally it was a San Francisco–based label that was pumping out a series of chart-hitting records. But the label always had deep connections in New Orleans. Master P was born in New Orleans's 3rd Ward, as he called out in his own song, "I'm Bout It." He produced New Orleans–based talent, Kane & Abel (then known as Double Vision), Mystikal, and TRU. TRU's album, *True,* reached gold status.

In 1995, Master P officially relocated No Limit to New Orleans, adding more New Orleans rappers to the lineup: Mia X, Fiend, Tre-8, and Mr. Serv-On. No Limit could have had its superstar in Soulja Slim, had the rapper not been shot and killed on Thanksgiving Day 2003. His first album, *Give It 2 'Em Raw,* debuted at #13 on the Billboard charts, having sold 82,000 in the first week. Soulja Slim was then convicted of armed robbery and incarcerated for three years. Released from prison, he recorded the album *The Streets Made Me* and hit the big time when his song "Slow Motion," recorded with Juvenile, became a #1 hit. "Slow Motion" has since grown to become a de facto stripper's anthem.

Cash Money Records was founded in 1991 by brothers Bryan "Birdman" Williams and Ronald "Slim" Williams. The brothers had the great insight or fortune to hire DJ Mannie Fresh as their in-house producer. Mannie had a distinctive approach to the Southern bass and mixed in a New Orleans sound: brass bands in the synthesizers, drum lines in the rattling beats, and Mardi Gras Indians in the call-and-response lyrics. Under Mannie's direction, Cash Money became an instant player with a succession of breakout hits. The music video for Juvenile's "Ha" featured a revolutionary look at the sometimes harsh life in New Orleans's Magnolia projects. His album *400 Degreez* sold 4.7 million copies. The Hot Boys, where Juvenile is partnered with Lil Wayne, B. G., and Turk became the label's big ticket. Their initial success with "Get It How U Live" set up a huge and lucrative distribution deal between Cash Money and Universal Records. It also inspired B. G., when describing the deal, to coin the phrase "bling bling"—a term that instantaneously permeated the culture.

Dwayne Michael Carter Jr. would be the Cash Money superstar. Known by his stage name Lil Wayne, he was the youngest artist on the label, starting as a 9-year-old and joining the Hot Boys at 15. His debut solo album, *Tha Block Is Hot,* was released when he was 17 and debuted at No. 3 on Billboard, going on to platinum. After a career of 13 best-selling albums, 8 lawsuits (including a $51 million suit he

filed against Cash Money), and 3 arrests, Lil Wayne announced he was exiting the music scene to spend more time with his four children.

Master P and No Limit Records did not exit the New Orleans scene in any better style. One of his first signed and top artists, Mystikal, was sentenced to six years in prison for sexual battery and extortion, and while incarcerated was charged with two counts of failing to file tax returns. Even worse, Master P did a stint on *Dancing with the Stars*.

Bounce, a style that grew out of rap and hip hop, is the hot new music . . . that's been around 25 years. The earliest bounce song can be traced back to a local duo, MC T. Tucker and DJ Irv, called "Fathers of Bounce." The two changed the course of New Orleans music with their 1991 local hit, "Where Dey At." MC T. Tucker and DJ Irv perfected and popularized the new music while working local clubs and selling tapes "out-the-trunk."

Bounce was characterized by a call-and-response delivery and the use of several fast-paced sampled tracks known as the "Triggerman beat" (also called "dat beat"). Bounce took over local clubs, bars, and school dances as quickly as Who Dat T-shirts. Its signature move occurs when a bounce artist yells, "hands on the floor" and the willing dancers collapse into an all-four position and start shaking their butts. You can think of it as a more music-centric version of twerking.

When the infectious, booty-shaking beat was picked up by Beyoncé, Katy Perry, and Adele, bounce became an international phenomena. Bounce music had been around New Orleans since the late 1980s (long before Beyoncé et al. picked up on it). In 2010, it got a burst of sudden attention when bounce rappers Big Freedia and Katey Red were profiled in *The New York Times* and *Vanity Fair*.

The New Orleans bounce artist Robert Maize, a.k.a. Mr. Ghetto, made a name for himself when his YouTube video "Walmart" went viral. Filmed with a handheld camera, it featured a couple of dancers popping (i.e., butt shaking) in a Walmart parking lot and in store aisles.

By the time Miley Cyrus lit up the Internet with her twerking performance on the MTV Awards, it was old news in New Orleans. Said Big Freedia, "I am excited about Miley twerking on the VMAs. She didn't twerk properly, but she opened the door for New Orleans and bounce music and myself." Locally, Big Freedia had issued "Azz Everywhere," his genre-shaping bounce classic a decade earlier.

On the worldwide scale, Big Freedia has undoubtedly become the face of bounce music, thanks mostly to his musical talent, plus his larger-than-life personality, and now a best-selling book and his reality TV show, *Big Freedia: Queen of Bounce*.

You would be mistaken to think that bounce is male dominated and misogynistic, like a lot of rap. There are in fact a number of female stars in the New Orleans scene. Of note is Mia X (should be XXX) who proves the point with the song "Funk You Up." Mia X has scripted some romantic lyrics like "Make the coochie scream for a six-inch stick? I pushed an eight-pound baby out, so that's bullshit." Her words, not mine.

The Diana Ross or Tina Turner of the rap scene in New Orleans has to be Cheeky Blakk. By day, she's Angela Woods, a nurse working in a retirement home. By night, she's Cheeky Blakk, songsmith of tunes like "Bitch Get Off Me," "Ride Fa My Nigga," and her massive hit "Twerk Something." She got into performing after an argument with the father of her child, Pimp Daddy Jenkins. He brought his anger to the stage, rapping a song with the line, "Here's another ho by the name of Cheeky

Blakk." Livid, she wrote her own song with the line, "Well, Pimp Daddy, it's about that time / Cheeky Blakk tell you 'bout your funny, fake-ass rhyme." Their airing of domestic issues became first class entertainment in the clubs. Pimp Daddy was later shot and killed. Her career, however, has continued to spiral upward. When asked by *OffBeat Magazine* why she's so successful, Cheeky Blakk answered, "Maybe it's because I touch people's penises when I go on stage."

For visitors looking to delve into the local bounce music scene, there are large-scale popping events at the Republic or House of Blues, and at smaller venues, such as the Siberia lounge. There are also drop-in bounce fitness classes, held at the Dancing Grounds community center in the Bywater neighborhood.

CHAPTER 13

Live Music Clubs, Dance Halls, Juke Joints, Bars,
Plus a Musical Laundromat

Live music is the cure for what ails ya. —**Henry Rollins**

During my research for this chapter, I stopped counting the number of live music venues in New Orleans when the list exceeded 100. With each venue offering performances anywhere from two to all seven nights a week, I would need to write a clause in my last will and testament to pass on the responsibility of finishing *Hear Dat* to my children, Austin or Ella, and possibly Cadence, my granddaughter. Entries here are arranged by neighborhood.

Bywater & The Marigny

Bacchanal Wine
600 Poland Ave.
Phone: 504-948-9111

Bacchanal opened as a neighborhood corner wine shop, right aside the Industrial Canal and the Mississippi River. After Hurricane Katrina, they opened up their back lot behind the 200-year-old building, where every Sunday night chefs who'd lost everything in the flood prepared dinners and kept their spirits alive. It became an iconic once-a-week event. Eventually, Bacchanal hired their own chef, Joaquin Rodas, and now serves seven nights a week.

Bacchanal is included here because you sit outdoors under strung lights and tiki torches and listen to live music by noted New Orleans musicians. The brilliant Helen Gillet, profiled elsewhere in this book, performs most Monday nights. Thursday nights is usually The Courtyard Kings, a group that merges bebop, gypsy jazz, Brazilian jazz, and New Orleans traditional jazz.

 BJ's Lounge
4301 Burgundy St.
Phone: 504-945-9256

BJ's is a bit frayed at the edges with yard sale chairs shoved against the wall next to an old upright piano I can only assume hasn't been tuned in decades, a wall of snapshots of former patrons, and torn-out pages from old *Playboy* magazines taped to the bathroom walls. The bar is and always will be cash only.

It's a perfect setting for the dirty blues of one of its regular performers, Little Freddie King. Every Monday night used to be King James & the Special Men, who brought their own red beans and rice. Since a few months ago, Mondays have belonged to one of the more unusually named bands in New Orleans, Lumpy Black Problem Variety Show: An Orgy of Remorse.

Cafe Istanbul
2372 St. Claude Ave.
Phone: 504-975-0286

Cafe Istanbul is the brain child of poet Chuck Perkins, who aims to foster and promote performance art in New Orleans. The nearly 4,000-square-foot theater with balcony space shows locally made movie premiers, comedy shows (most notably the Goodnight Show with John Calhoun, which is basically a New Orleans take on *A Prairie Home Companion*), dance troupes, and live music. The cafe (without food) has recently hosted the Bad Boyz of R&B, the 10th Anniversary Mantra Music Concert, and NOLA Jam Session.

Checkpoint Charlie
501 Esplanade Ave.
Phone: 504-281-4847

The name of the place is actually Igor's Checkpoint Charlie, but no one calls it that. Alongside the French Quarter, at the mouth of Frenchmen Street, Checkpoint Charlie is a hangout that can meet almost all your needs with its bar, pool table, pinball machines, wash and dry machines, passable half-pound Charlie burgers, jalapeño poppers, mini-pizzas, chicken nuggets, or cheese fries, and a small stage where you can hear rock, metal, or punk, depending on the night. Just don't use the bathrooms. A Yelp text commented that they "would be considered a disgrace in most 3rd world countries."

Regular bands include Bible Belt Sinners, Bad Moon Lander, and The Olivia deHavilland Mosquitoes, all bands you're not likely to see anywhere else. Tuesday evenings are the well-attended open mic blues jam.

Vaughan's Lounge
4229 Dauphine St.
Phone: (504) 947-5562

For more than 20 years, Kermit Ruffins's Thursday night sessions at Vaughan's were an iconic event in New Orleans. An entire book, Jay Mazza's *Not Just Another Thursday Night,* was written about the weekly party. After opening his own club, Ruffins felt it was time for a change. This beautifully dilapidated corner bar still draws crowds for other performers, The Heart Attacks, The Southern BarBitchurates, and the approaching stardom of Corey Henry and The Treme Funktet.

The French Quarter

Balcony Music Club
1331 Decatur St.
Phone: 504-301-5912

More often called BMC, there's almost always a barker out front trying to syphon off the stream of nighthawks headed right across the street toward Frenchmen's gauntlet of music clubs. There's never a cover for the seven nights of music: jazz, funk, but most often blues.

The Bombay Club
830 Conti St.
Phone: 504-577-2237

Having the look and feel of a British hunt club with deep leather chairs, bronze equestrian statues, and a grandfather clock, The Bombay Club is appreciably different from any other place in New Orleans where you might take in live music. They are first and foremost an upscale restaurant that features noted chef Nathan Richard. An essential part of the meal is their lineup of musicians. They serve jazz: pianists like Kris Tokarski and Tom Hook, jazz guitarists like Matt Johnson, and singers like Linnzi Zaorski and Banu Gibson. Occasionally they step ever-so-slightly outside the pure jazz lineup with Latin jazz (Los Tres Amigos).

The Carousel Bar
214 Royal St. (Hotel Monteleone)
Phone: 504-523-3341

The Carousel Bar is situated at the front of the historic (and haunted) Hotel Monteleone. The slowly rotating bar has been a local legend since 1949 (the hotel's been around since 1888).

The music aligns with the elegance of the setting. Their weekly lineup is built around contemporary jazz masters. Thursdays, ex-Chicagoan Nayo Jones sings; Fridays will be modern jazz singer Robin Barnes and/or Lena Prima, daughter of the legendary Louis Prima; Saturdays showcase Luther Kent, who mixes swing blues with R&B; and Tom Hook, a former floating lounge lizard who performed on the *Mississippi Queen* for many years.

Chris Owens Club
500 Bourbon St.
Phone: 504-523-6400

This club is the lone remaining remnant from Bourbon Street's glory days. The ageless Ms. Owens has been hitting the stage in sequins and feathers since the 1960s. Her high energy and higher kitsch-value shows are most often accompanied by her Latin Rhythms band, but she's integrated all types of music into her act, including bounce. An evening at Chris Owens is the equivalent to taking in a Vegas show with Wayne Newton or Tom Jones.

The Davenport Lounge
921 Canal St. (The Ritz-Carlton)
Phone: 504-524-1331

Located in the Ritz-Carlton, the lounge is named after its headliner, Jeremy Davenport, a jazz trumpeter and vocalist. The scene is appropriately elegant, maybe even swanky. Live jazz is offered on Wednesdays and Thursdays from 5:30 p.m. to 9:30 p.m., and Fridays and Saturdays from 9:00 p.m. to 1:00 a.m.

The Famous Door
339 Bourbon St.
Phone: 504-598-4334

Longtime Bourbon St. impresario John Wehner presents R&B and dance bands seven nights a week. It claims to be the oldest live music venue on Bourbon Street, open since 1934.

Fritzel's European Jazz Club
733 Bourbon St.
Phone: 504-586-4800

Fritzel's is a classic jazz club that's been in the heart of the Bourbon Street madness since the early 1960s. They claim to be the city's oldest operating jazz club. There's a lot of claiming going on. Dixieland jazz is served near the fireplace or on the patio, along with imported beers or cocktails doused with European schnapps.

Funky Pirate Blues Club
727 Bourbon St.
Phone: 504-523-1960

Practically next door to Fritzel's, the Funky Pirate serves as the longtime home for Big Al Carson and The Blues Masters. The 495-pound blues and funk musician with the velvety voice has been performing on their tiny stage every Thursday through Saturday night for more than 20 years. On other nights the Funky Pirate features long sets of raunchy blues.

House of Blues
225 Decatur St.
Phone: 504-529-2583

Both a solid restaurant and live music venue, House of Blues has hosted famous musicians from New Orleans (Fats Domino, Trombone Shorty, and Dr. John) and beyond (Ziggy Marley, Lady Gaga, and Eric Clapton). Every Sunday morning House of Blues has a rousing Gospel Brunch.

Irvin Mayfield's Jazz Playhouse
300 Bourbon St. (The Royal Sonesta Hotel)
Phone: 504-553-2299

Recently, I've had a hard time recommending Irvin Mayfield's club. The music is just as good as ever. Regulars like jazz singer Germaine Bazzle and Gerald French and the Original Tuxedo Jazz Band remain "should sees"; and Trixie Minx, our premier burlesque queen, I'd rate close to a "must see" for her performances every Friday at midnight. My issue is with the club's namesake and Grammy Award–winning jazz trumpet player, and former Cultural Ambassador of the City of New Orleans, Irvin Mayfield. He deserves to be profiled in this book. You'll note he is not. Post Katrina, he managed the New Orleans Public Library system and managed to pay himself a six-figure salary, and is currently under FBI investigation for allegedly funneling more than $850,000 from donations to the library's private fundraising to his own New Orleans Jazz Orchestra.

One Eyed Jacks
615 Toulouse St.
Phone: 504-569-8361

Rich in history, One Eyed Jacks is a former movie palace. It then became the epicenter for the rebirth of burlesque in New Orleans, was home of the Shim Shamettes, and is now an eclectic, bordello-feeling club that hosts a variety of musical pleasures.

The front room bar, the original lobby, looks like a Russian Tea Room with embossed burgundy wallpaper and chandeliers. The second room features a performance stage with a large round bar. And the balcony bar upstairs is kitsch central, lined with velvet paintings and lamps in the shape of matadors.

The music offerings range the gambit from rock, including '80s large-haired glam rock, metal, national performers like The White Stripes, burlesque shows, and more. It is the ideal setting for The Bingo Show, which takes the stage every so often. The club's locally famous Fast Times '80s Dance Party happens every Thursday night and features live go-go dancers.

Palm Court
1204 Decatur St.
Phone: 504-525-0200

Palm Court opened in 1989 as a dinner jazz club. The in-house jazz orchestra is filled with venerable musicians. Headliner Lionel Ferbos died in 2014. He was 103 years old and played cornet with the band up to within a week of his passing. Though, quite honestly, sometimes when the 100-plus-year-old musician sat in with the band, he literally just sat with the band. In an effort to sell themselves, Palm Court was quick to point out to me, "We still have two 90-year-olds in the band."

Warehouse District

Circle Bar
1032 St. Charles Ave.
Phone: 504-588-2616

Standing (barely . . . with peeling walls and warped floors) in the shadow of Robert E. Lee's statue on Lee Circle, the bar was originally the office of Dr. Elizabeth Magus Cohen. She was the first female licensed physician in Louisiana. She came to New Orleans in 1857 to work with patients who were suffering through epidemics of smallpox and yellow fever.

The tiny music room inside can cure what ails you between the hours of 9:00 p.m. till 4:00 a.m.

The names of the constantly changing bands alone reveal the types of music played there: Gramps The Vamp, Barb Wire Dolls, The Quintessential Octopus, and Those Folks with the Hokum High Rollers. Hint: None play Dixieland or Top 40 hits.

The Howlin' Wolf
907 So. Peters St.
Phone: 504-522-9653

Opened in 1988 in an old cotton warehouse, The Howlin' Wolf outgrew the space and they moved into what was previously the New Orleans Music Hall. Outside is a mural masterpiece created by artist Michalopoulos that depicts our music history from Louis Armstrong to a second line with the Dirty Dozen Brass Band. Inside, the bar comes from Al Capone's hotel in Chicago. It was dismantled there and reassembled here. The black curtains on stage were salvaged from the Orpheum theatre.

Over the years, The Howlin' Wolf has hosted the Foo Fighters, The Meters, Wu-Tang Clan, Dr. John, and Death Cab For Cutie. It is the every-Sunday-night home for the Grammy-nominated Hot 8 Brass Band. They occasionally have burlesque, and twice a week they showcase comedians: Comedy Beast on Tuesdays and Comedy Gumbeaux on Thursdays.

Little Gem Saloon

445 Rampart St.
Phone: 504-267-4863

Little Gem Saloon is the first and, currently, the only restoration in the neighborhood that experts consider vital for the development of jazz. In the early 1900s, the then-sketchy area, bordering Storyville's red light district, was booze, jazz, and brothels. It was called "Back o Town" and was the hub for African American social life in New Orleans with the restaurant menus and musical styles that catered to those tastes.

Little Gem Saloon dinner jazz club opened in 1903 under kingpin Frank Doroux. He also owned the Eagle Saloon, practically next door. The Iroquois Theater was on the same block. Jazz greats Joseph "King" Oliver, Jelly Roll Morton, Sidney Bechet, Kid Ory, and Buddy Bolden got their starts playing at these clubs. As a young boy, Louis Armstrong won a talent contest at the Iroquois by covering his face in flour and doing a "white face" routine.

Beginning in the 1920s, major changes dried up the neighborhood. The US government shut down legalized prostitution. Said New Orleans mayor Martin Behrman, "You can make it illegal, but you can't make it unpopular." The second death blow came with the explosion of movie houses on Canal Street, which syphoned off the customers from vaudeville and live jazz. The last of the clubs closed in 1927. Little Gem Saloon became a loan office. And the final blow came after Katrina, when, in a rush to rebuild, city officials unwittingly approved the demolition of the childhood home of jazz great Sidney Bechet and the Iroquois Theater.

Dr. Nicolas Bazan with his son, daughter, and son-in-law bought Little Gem Saloon in 2012 and set out to restore the venue. The space had been boarded up for the previous 40 years. And more than 100 years after Little Gem first opened, it again opened for business. Little Gem is today an intimate and relaxed dinner jazz club. Regular performers include Kermit Ruffins (most Saturdays), Nayo Jones (most Fridays), and the Messy Cookers Jazz Band (most Tuesdays).

Republic
828 So. Peters St.
Phone: 504-528-8282

The 150-year-old building, once a coffee warehouse, has been converted into a spacious (a 2,500-square-foot mezzanine hovers over a 4,000-square-foot dance floor), uber-hip setting with Art Deco murals, vintage brick walls, large slate bar, crystal chandeliers, and exposed wooden beams. It also comes with a New York/LA attitude befitting the space. If you aren't "somebody" or you aren't friends with the bouncers, you'll wait in line to get in. Unless, of course, you've bought their VIP package (generally $35–100, depending on who's playing) whereby you skip the line, get exclusive seating, bottle service, and your own personal cocktail server.

DJ-themed bounce nights and Throwback nights occur on weekends. The club also features live performances with nationally known artists like Juvenile and Naughty By Nature, or up-and-comers like Unknown Mortal Orchestra and Girlpool and Alex G.

Tremé

Candlelight Lounge
925 No. Robertson St.
Phone: 504-525-4748

Located in the historic Tremé, the Candlelight Lounge is an often-packed neighborhood dive that features live music, brass bands, bold drinks, and lively times. It's also a favorite end point for second line parades. The Treme Brass Band plays there every Wednesday night.

The Ooh Poo Pah Doo Bar
1931 Orleans Ave.
Phone: 504-435-3384

Judy and Brian Broadus opened the club on Halloween day 2013 as a tribute to her musical family and a place to help preserve and inspire live music in Tremé. The bar is named after the 1960 hit song by Judy's father, the late R&B legend Jessie Hill. Hill's grandsons include trumpeter James Andrews (dubbed "Satchmo of the Ghetto"), James's brother Troy "Trombone Shorty" Andrews, and their cousins Travis "Trumpet Black" Hill (who died in 2015 at the age of 28) and Glen David Andrews. While the bar is home for the clan, other musicians are welcomed. Grammy-nominated artist Guitar Slim Jr. plays many weekends. The Ooh Poo Pah Doo has weekly jam sessions with Mardi Gras Indians.

Mid-City

Banks Street Bar & Grill
4401 Banks St.
Phone: 504-486-0258

This is a tiny little watering hole populated mostly by indigenous peoples. The music is a rotation of regional funk, blues, and rock bands every night. Ron Hotstream and The F-Holes are semi-regulars. There's no cover. Better than no cover, Banks Street serves free red beans and rice on Mondays and free oysters on Thursday nights after 10:00 p.m.

Chickie Wah Wah
2828 Canal St.
Phone: 504-304-4714

Both the City Park and Cemeteries streetcar lines on the Canal stop directly in front of Chickie Wah Wah, making it one of the most convenient clubs for visitors without cars. The problem would be if you happened not to like the musicians on stage, because it's located in a nightlife no-man's land. Chickie Wah Wah is nestled between a Harley dealer and a blood donation clinic.

Fortunately, Chickie Wah Wah has secured a solid schedule of New Orleans's premier performers. For me, Meschiya Lake and Tom McDermott on Tuesday nights is the "must." But for others, John Rankin (Wednesdays), or Jon Cleary (when he's in town) could easily fulfill that role. "The Punk Empress of African Rock," Cole Williams, is new to New Orleans, is already wowing audiences with her music, and is described as African rock meets Jamaican soul. Chickie Wah Wah generously gives the performers 100 percent of the door each night.

At the front of the club is Blue Oak BBQ, which some (well . . . at least me) consider to be the best barbecue in the city.

Gentilly

Bullet's Sports Bar
2441 A P Tureaud Ave.
Phone: 504-948-4003

Bullet's was regularly used as a setting on the HBO series *Treme*. Prior to their newfound "fame," it was very much a neighborhood joint, off the beaten track, and inhabited exclusively by locals. They offer R&B (five different R&B bands play on Sundays, starting at 7 p.m.), brass band (the all-girl brass band Pinettes performs on Fridays), and Kermit Ruffins & the Barbecue Swingers on Tuesdays. Food trucks line up outside during live shows.

Uptown and Carrollton

Carrollton Station Bar & Music Club
8140 Willow St.
Phone: 504-865-9190

This neighborhood bar and music club is a bit out of the way for most visitors. Located at the end of the St. Charles Streetcar line, the bar has events like open mic comedy (Wednesdays), live trivia (Thursdays), and the occasional ping pong tournament, none of which will make the destination worth the journey. One dollar taco night (Fridays) is a bit more inviting. They have 10 beers on tap and a signature drink, the Electric Blueberry Moonshine Lemonade. But the reason to go is the music on Friday and Saturday nights. They've hosted some of our best, like Little Freddie King and Debauche: Russian Mafia Band.

Dos Jefes Uptown Cigar Bar
5535 Tchoupitoulas St.
Phone: 504-891-8500

This is not a typical cigar bar where guys, desperate to be like Arnold Schwarzenegger or Sly Stallone, sit around posing with stogies in ways they practiced at home in front of a mirror.

It's become known for one of the best assortments of fine liquor in NOLA, and features top-notch live music six nights a week. Regulars include Joe Krown, Sunpie Barnes, gypsy swing from the Courtyard Kings, and Latin jazz from Rick Trolsen's Gringo do Choro.

Gasa Gasa
4920 Freret St.
Phone: 504-304-7110

Gasa Gasa is a funky art house that hosts weekly art exhibitions, film screenings, and live music shows. They sometimes host name musicians like Walter "Wolfman" Washington, but more often have alternative bands like Royal T with Painted Hands and Vapo Rats or Hydrogen Child with Bantam Foxes & Von Mozes. Each week Gasa Gasa has Cornhole Thursdays in the courtyard.

Le Bon Temps Roule
4801 Magazine St.
Phone: 504-895-8117

In addition to being a New Orleans signature phrase (it means "Let the Good Times Roll"), Le Bon Temps Roule is a rowdy and revered neighborhood bar. The bar and pool tables are upfront. The music stage, called "House of Dues" (because it's where local bands pay their dues before being discovered), is in back. The music is everything from brass bands to klezmer. The night to go is Thursday when the Soul Rebels play each week, though free oysters are on Fridays and dollar beers are served during Saints games.

Off the Map (literally and figuratively)

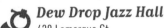

Dew Drop Jazz Hall
430 Lamarque St.
Mandeville, Louisiana

Getting there is a bit of an adventure that will require you to cross the Causeway Bridge over Lake Pontchartrain (the world's longest bridge over a body of water—24 miles). The trip is totally worth the effort. On the other side of the lake is the town of Old Mandeville, and the Dew Drop is the oldest jazz hall in America (1895). Back in the early 1900s, New Orleans jazz pioneers, after playing more traditional music for whites-only audiences, would rush across the lake where they'd cut loose for black audiences who were receptive to their newfangled sounds. Dew Drops's performers represent a who's who of jazz greats: Kid Ory, Bunk Johnson, the Fitz Brothers Band, Buddy Mandalay, George Lewis, Buddie Petit, and, most notably, Louie Armstrong, who played there often.

Today, the Dew Drop hosts two to four performances a month (check their website for a schedule: www.dewdropjazzhall.com). If you go, be prepared to step back into time. Very little has changed since Bunk Johnson and Louis Armstrong played there. It looks like an old country church, has no air conditioning or heating, no insulation, no running water, and no restrooms (you can use the building next door). Electricity is provided by a single line that powers multicolored bare bulbs to light the room. The room itself can seat 100 people uncomfortably on wooden benches without backs.

Admission is $10 and is sold only in person. Next door sells $10 fried chicken or catfish dinners with rice and beans, potato salad, and cornbread that is prepared by the ladies of the First Free Mission Baptist Church. Dinner is served in Styrofoam boxes meant for your lap. Everything is cash only.

The beatitude you'll experience is free. My wife and I were literally in tears as a 70-something couple executed a perfect Cajun waltz down the aisle as Helen Gillet played from a tiny stage upfront. As said by Dew Drop performer Deacon John, "The best thing about playing at a historic venue like this is that you feel the spirits permeating the room. When I get in here, I feel like my ancestors are playing backup."

Ryan Hodgson-Rigsbee

WWOZ

When you visit New Orleans or live in New Orleans, 90.7 on your FM dial is the soundtrack of the city. Their stated mission is to be the worldwide authentic voice, archive, and flag-bearer of New Orleans culture.

Brothers Walter and Jerry Brock arrived in New Orleans from Texas in the 1970s with a massive record collection of New Orleans musicians, from Jelly Roll Morton to Dr. John. When they got here, they were amazed (Allen Toussaint might have said they got stomped) by the richness of the music they heard in the local clubs and bars and on the street. It was way beyond their collection. At that time local music was barely heard on the radio, except maybe a few classic songs around Mardi Gras.

Also at that time radio stations across the country were being snapped up and turned into Casey Kasem insipidness. The Brock brothers wanted the music, and not the on-air personalities, to be the focus of their station. The call letters WWOZ were chosen as a reference to the Wizard of Oz, as in "Pay no attention to the man behind the curtain." What was important was New Orleans music.

The station started out small, one might say spartan. In the earliest days WWOZ operated out of the upstairs beer storage room at Tipitina's. Often the DJs would drop a microphone through a hole in the floor and broadcast the live music playing on the stage below. The upstairs studio had no air-conditioning and, for a time, the only running water was from a neighbor's garden hose that was run in through a window. Everyone who worked there did additional tasks as a volunteer, be it addressing envelopes, sweeping the floor, or doing whatever else needed to be done.

The brothers got to know local artists through well-placed and connected new friends. Rickie Castrillo, a musician and stage manager at the club Rosy's, made sure they met and would play on air Irma Thomas, Earl King, and other R&B greats. Danny Barker was their guide to traditional jazz.

During this time, in addition to getting up to speed on the musicians, they had the arduous task of getting a broadcast permit. The Brock brothers formed the nonprofit Nora Blatch Educational Foundation, named after a female engineer and radio pioneer. They then had to negotiate the complexities of getting a federal license. It took them four years of fundraising, ground work, paperwork, and legal hearings to finally be awarded a federal permit on December 4, 1980.

WWOZ was on the air within 24 hours later. For the first weeks, the Brocks would tape programs at home and race out to the transmitter shack to get them on the air. The broadcasts weren't just spinning records, they were also featuring interviews and live on-air performances by James Booker, Dave Bartholomew, Ernie K-Doe, and other local legends. Ernie K-Doe was even given his own weekly program, *Burn, K-Doe, Burn!*, where he got to speak extemporaneously about whatever passed through his unpredictable mind.

WWOZ was not only *not* your father's radio station, it wasn't your dentist's, accountant's, or weird uncle's. It was a thing unto itself. Jason Berry, in his excellent book, *Up From the Cradle of Jazz*, called WWOZ "the most exciting broadcast development of the 1980s. It became a kaleidoscope of voices, rich in oral imagery—jazzmen, composers, Cajun fiddlers, parades, grand marshals, gospel artists and R&B bluesmen, writers, occasional filmmakers, historians, Mardi Gras Indians, fathers and sons and mothers and daughters of musical families. WWOZ provided intimacy between the musicians and listeners, immeasurably broadening the sense of place."

In 1984, WWOZ moved out of the cramped space above Tipitina's and into what must have felt like Shangri-La—a three-room office in Louis Armstrong Park. Three years later, the financially strapped Nora Blatch Educational Foundation turned the station's license over to the Friends of WWOZ, a not-for-profit established by the New Orleans Jazz & Heritage Festival Foundation.

The Foundation and local support has made it possible for the station to grow from the Brock brothers beautiful idea to what is now widely recognized as one of the best radio stations in the country. *Rolling Stone* magazine in their feature "The 125-Plus People, Places and Things Ruling the Rock and Roll Universe," named WWOZ one of the top radio stations in the country. *Esquire* honored them as the Internet Radio Station of the Year, saying that this "resilient miracle of FM radio plays funk, jazz, blues, roots, Latin, soul, zydeco, R&B, and everything in between."

WWOZ has given and continues to give New Orleans two gifts. One is their Livewire Music Calendar that outlines who's playing where tonight (or any upcoming night). You can access it online at their website (www.wwoz.org), and DJs announce at least the current night's lineup several times on air each day. *OffBeat*, a free monthly magazine, also lists performances on its back pages. On average, you can expect to have a good 100 live performers from which to choose each day. Seriously, I just checked today's calendar and counted 103. Tomorrow night, 112.

WWOZ's other lasting gift is Davis Rogan. Depending on your perspective, he is our oversized, overly energetic Falstaff, comically getting in your space with his large 6-foot-4-inch frame and flailing arms as he expostulates his passionately held opinions. Or he could be viewed as a New

Orleans version of Randy Newman, a bigger, messier songsmith who replaces "I Love L.A." and "Short People" with his parody of post-Katrina recovery, "The New 9th Ward," and a song about the failures of it all, "A Road Home." Or, from yet a third point of view, Davis Rogan could be seen as a real-life musical version of the New Orleans fictional hero, Ignatius P. Reilly of *Confederacy of Dunces*. He is, no matter your slant or your chosen handle, a force or a farce to be reckoned with.

To be fair, Davis Rogan was a below-the-radar, kinda-sorta-known musician well before WWOZ. He played in a '90s funk-rap band named All That. But, it was his 13 years of live-time pandemonium on air as a host on WWOZ that brought him fully to New Orleans's attention. He did eventually wear out his welcome and was dismissed for (A) his "tardiness, erratic, and sometimes disruptive behavior," as stated by program director Dwayne Breashears, or (B) that he spilled a giant-size bottle of soda over the station's soundboard, or (C) the most commonly held belief: that he was grounded because of his rebellious insistence on playing bounce music, at the time forbidden at WWOZ. Regardless of the real reason, it's almost a badge of honor to be fired from the radio station that allowed host Bob French to wander off on air with long diatribes during his show, *French Cooking*, and where Ernie K-Doe blasted unfiltered stream of consciousness from whatever came into his frenzied mind during his classic radio show, *Burn, K-Doe, Burn!*.

Rogan has also been shown the door and occasionally banned from other establishments for his undisciplined rants and exploits. His transgressions run the gambit from berating customers or bartenders at a high volume, to dropping his pants when a stronger point needs to be made. At d.b.a., the club on Frenchmen, there's a posted sign that reads, "If your name is Davis Rogan, please leave."

I'm half afraid Davis Rogan will read this book and come after me for leaving out some of his favorite bands like A Tribe Called Quest, The Roots, and The Pharcyde, or for expressing an opinion with which he passionately disagrees. All of his opinions are passionate.

If this all sounds vaguely or overtly familiar, Steve Zahn's character in HBO's *Treme*, Davis McAlary, is based directly upon the real-life Davis Rogan. Director David Simon heard of, then met, then fell for his "Davey-ness." Said Simon, "Like New Orleans, Davis Rogan is always one bad move away from falling on his ass. And yet, on at least every other occasion, he's the cat that drops from the tree and lands on his feet. Much as New Orleans somehow manages to do." Rogan was hired to help write episodes of the TV series, including about his fictional self.

CONCLUSION

Every time I close my eyes blowing the trumpet of mine—I look right in the heart of good old New Orleans. It has given me something to live for.

—Louis Armstrong

New Orleans music is so real and so human. It sounds so much like life.

—Jon Batiste

More than sound and story, New Orleans music has soul, in the larger nonmusical sense. As local news anchor Rob Nelson has said, "New Orleans is straight soul with no chaser."

During my first year living in New Orleans, one of my key missions was to build a putt-putt course. The two courses that had been here in town were both wiped out by Hurricane Katrina. My then-9-year-old daughter was distraught. Ignoring our incomparable food, music, rich history, beautiful weather, lush vegetation, and the friendliest, most chat-filled people on the planet, she complained, "No putt-putt?"

I told her I'd take care of it. I met with the City Planning Commission and the Bywater Neighborhood Association. I then brought down two incredibly creative people from New York to help me visualize the course. Maria Reidelbach, a public, dumpster-diving artist, may be the leading authority on miniature golf in the country. She designed a putt-putt course on a pier in New York City (that Rudy "No Fun" Giuliani later tore down) and designed another still-standing one near New Paltz, New York, with Gnome Chompsky, the world's largest garden gnome statue. She also literally wrote the book on putt-putt. *Miniature Golf* is a classic book, if only for its memorable Astro Turf cover. Her then-boyfriend, Chris Butler, is probably best known for his 1980s classic pop song, "I Know What Boys Like." He is less well known for currently living in the house where Jeffrey Dahmer grew up and allegedly made his first kill.

After their first week ever in New Orleans, these two creative souls were completely seduced by the city's charms. Said Chris, "New Orleans is just like New York City in the '60s and '70s. All this creative energy and it's not about making money or being a brand. It's like, 'Sounds like fun. Let's do it.'"

And that's the essence of the New Orleans music scene. It comes from a real place. It comes from the heart. Whether it's our music royalty like Dr. John, or Helen Gillet on her cello, Little Freddie King playing his blues guitar, Amanda Shaw on her fiddle, Washboard Chaz strumming his metal washboard vest, or Quintron creating strange beats on his Drum Buddy, the music here is born from and executed with an absolutely bona fide foundation.

Said Ian Neville of growing up here, "Being a child in New Orleans, you're naturally exposed to music in ways you aren't anywhere else. Parades, marching bands, second lines, the sounds of the streets, the chants of the Mardi Gras Indians. My great uncle was Big Chief Jolly of the Wild Tchoupitoulas. My father and all my uncles were musicians. I met Allan Toussaint and Earl King and Dr. John when I was a kid. All of it was inspiration, available for us to soak up."

Pete Fountain echoes, "If I had grown up in any place but New Orleans, I don't think my career would have taken off. I wouldn't have heard the music that was around this town. There was so much going on when I was a kid."

My favorite scene from the HBO series *Treme* came when Steve Zahn's character, Davis McAlary, kept pestering Kermit Ruffins to leave the stage and go introduce himself to Elvis Costello, who was sitting at a table in the juke joint.

Frustrated, Steve Zahn's character finally hammered, "Is all you wanna do is get high, play music in New Orleans, and eat barbecue?" Ruffins's perfect response: "That'll work."

If you weren't born here, as I was not, you can still come to New Orleans if just to visit and devour our music as you would our gumbo, dressed po'boys, and chargrilled oysters. Or do both, being mesmerized by Helen Gillet while eating bacon-wrapped dates at Bacchanal, or BBQ from Blue Oak while listening to Meschiya Lake and Tom McDermott at Chickie Wah Wah, or the baked oyster casserole at Little Gem Saloon while Kermit Ruffins himself plays his trumpet. Do so and you'll know exactly what Kermit meant. That'll work.

What happens in Vegas may stay in Vegas, but what happens in New Orleans, goes home with you.

—Laurell K. Hamilton

APPENDIX A
FESTIVALS AND FREE CONCERTS

If you're planning a trip to New Orleans, you might want to build it around one of our many festivals. If you have no choice for when you visit and must adhere to a conference or convention date, check the festival schedule, there's a good chance that a festival will be taking place while you are in town.

March

French Quarter Festival

Free music is played by the best New Orleans has to offer on various stages placed throughout the Quarter. Inexpensive sample dishes prepared by top restaurants are sold from adjoining tents. I hear that years ago this was a fabulous weekend where you could grab a lawn chair and stroll the French Quarter to take in a variety of musicians. The festival has grown since then, and now draws a half-million attendees. Last year, I looked forward to seeing Dr. John in one of his rare live appearances. So did thousands and thousands of others. Not being able to see and barely able to hear Dr. John, I tiptoed over coolers and seated music lovers to squirm my way out.

Wednesday at the Square

Free music on Wednesday evenings, 5:30–8:00 p.m., at Lafayette Square in the Warehouse District. Concerts run March through June.

BUKU Music + Art Project

One of the newer events to the New Orleans festival scene, BUKU is a progressive music and arts festival that features local and national artists such as The Flaming Lips, David Guetta, Ellie Goulding. It is held at Mardi Gras World, a popular sight-seeing destination. The festival also offers the opportunity to paint on the Graffiti Wall, view local art exhibitions, and eat local cuisine.

Soul Fest

Celebrating the legacy of African American food, music, and culture, this festival draws more than 20,000 people to the Audubon Zoo. Live performances are given by local jazz, rhythm and blues, and gospel artists. Food includes fried Louisiana alligator kabobs.

Congo Square New World Rhythms Festival

The New Orleans Jazz & Heritage Foundation puts on the Congo Square New World Rhythms Festival in Louis Armstrong Park. This free event celebrates the cultural diversity of New Orleans and the melting pot of traditions that gave rise to our unique music.

April

Jazz & Heritage Festival

The granddaddy of all New Orleans music festivals is always the last weekend in April and first weekend in May. Thursdays, being less crowded, are the best days to go. There are always five or more stages of live music going at any one time. The food, like Mango Freezes and Crawfish Monica, is as much the headliner as the musicians. Most A-list performers understand the importance of this event and bring their best. Bruce Springsteen usually delivers three-hour sets. Although A-listers like Springsteen, The Who, Tony Bennett, and Lenny Kravitz may impress you, it's the groups you may not have heard, like Earphunk, the Storyville Stompers Brass Band, or Cynthia Girtley, the Gospel Diva, who will blow you away.

ChazFest

Washboard Chaz lent his name to this Jazz Fest alternative. Held the same opening weekend as Jazz Fest, it is held at the Truck Farm (3020 St. Claude). ChazFest features some lesser-known artists along with some of our best, like Helen Gillet, King James and the Special Men, and the Tin Men.

May

Ponderosa Stomp

The Ponderosa Stomp is sponsored by The Mystic Knights of the Mau Mau, a charitable organization dedicated to preserving and presenting the rich history of American roots music. Held at House of Blues in the French Quarter, the event celebrates unsung heroes and heroines of rock and roll, rhythm and blues, and other forms of American roots music while those artists are still alive. Past Stomps have showcased Sam the Sham, the Sun Ra Orchestra, Robert Jr. Lockwood, Roy Head, Bobby Rush, and Elvis's drummer.

Mid-City Bayou Boogaloo

From jazz and blues to Cajun and country, three days of free live music bring more than 20,000 people to the banks of the beautiful Bayou St. John.

June

Cajun-Zydeco Festival

If you are one of the visitors looking for Cajun and zydeco music, June is when to come. Louis Armstrong Park hosts the annual festival that draws some of the bigger names like BeauSoleil, Michael Doucet, and Jo-El Sonnier.

Wednesdays on the Point

For a $2 ferry ride, you can cross the Mississippi River to partake of a free concert series that runs from June through August. Performers are all name musicians. A recent lineup included Amanda Shaw, Rebirth Brass Band, and Big Chief Monk Boudreaux.

Essence Music Festival

This is a huge star-studded celebration of African American music and culture with performances in the Mercedes-Benz Superdome and the Convention Center. Each year brings a half-million visitors to see the biggest hip hop, R&B, and soul artists. Expect performances by the likes of Aretha Franklin, Prince, Usher, Mary J. Blige, Beyoncé, the Pointer Sisters, Kanye West, Earth, Wind & Fire . . . and I could go on.

August

Satchmo SummerFest

Each year, this weekend-long festival celebrates the life, legacy, and music of Louis Armstrong. The festivities include a seminar series, jazz exhibitions, a jazz mass and second-line parade, and a host of star-studded performers.

September

Jazz in the Park

Free music returns to Louis Armstrong Park from September till November. The series features our best musicians from a wide range of styles: John Boutté, the Soul Rebels, Rockin' Dopsie, the Wild Tchoupitoulas, and the great Irma Thomas.

Harvest the Music

Free music returns to Lafayette Square in September and October. Legendary performers like The Iguanas, Anders Osborne, and Dr. John give it up at no cost.

October

Crescent City Blues & BBQ Festival

The event, which is another New Orleans Jazz & Heritage Foundation-sponsored festival, is held in Lafayette Square Park. The music is focused on blues, and the food is obviously all about the BBQ.

Voodoo Music + Arts Experience

This Halloween-themed festival in City Park blends hard rock and metal. Big-name acts like Ozzy Osbourne, Marilyn Manson, 50 Cent, Red Hot Chili Peppers, Nine Inch Nails, R.E.M., and 311, mix with local Louisiana musicians, including the original Meters, Trombone Shorty, and Dr. John.

Ogden After Hours

Throughout the year, Ogden Museum of Southern Art sponsors a series of music performances. Musicians play 6:00–8:00 p.m., 50 nights a year. The cost is $10 for nonmembers and is free for members of the museum.

There are many free concert series in New Orleans. Think about the quality of musicians who perform. It'd be as though you could wander into Central Park or Washington Square and see Jay Z, Bruce Springsteen, Lady Gaga, and Vampire Weekend—for free.

WHERE TO BUY STUFF

Louisiana Music Factory is first in the list because it is the unofficial record store of New Orleans. Other entries are listed here alphabetically.

Louisiana Music Factory
421 Frenchmen St., Faubourg Marigny
Phone: 504-586-1094
Hours: Sun.–Thurs.: 11:00 a.m.–8:00 p.m., Fri. and Sat.: 11:00 a.m.–10:00 p.m.
Barry Smith, onetime booking agent for Tipitina's with an MBA from Loyola, and Jerry Brock, a former petroleum engineer who cofounded WWOZ radio, met while working as over-qualified clerks at Record Ron's. Rather than talking about the latest Jim Jarmusch film or arguing the merits of guitarists Jeff Beck versus Jimmy Page, they instead concocted a plan to open their own record store.

In 1992, their Louisiana Music Factory opened on North Peters, which today houses Coyote Ugly Saloon. Smith remembers, "We started with a very small private loan and people close to us were skeptical that there wasn't enough business to go around with Tower Records and other stores in the area." Four years later, they needed more space and moved to Decatur Street.

Today Tower Records is gone and Peaches Records is hanging on by a well-worn thread. Louisiana Music Factory has become one of the most respected record stores in the country and one of the hubs in the New Orleans music scene. They moved for a third time in 2014 and are now housed amidst the music clubs lining Frenchmen Street. The new location has Swamp Shop, a kiosk-size store within the store that sells WWOZ paraphernalia and collectibles. The store has an extensive stock of indigenous music: jazz, blues, zydeco, Cajun, swamp pop, brass band, on both CDs and vinyl. There are many listening stations in the store and the place is staffed by exceptionally knowledgeable clerks, some whom have worked there since shortly after Earth cooled.

Domino Sound
2557 Bayou Rd.
Phone: 504-309-0871
Hours: Wed.–Mon.: noon–6:00 p.m.
Domino Sound carries new and used vinyl records, cassettes, dominoes, and some stereo equipment, including turntables. The store has well-stocked selections of

punk, blues, jazz, soul, hip hop, rock, folk, avant-garde, and local musicians. They claim to have the largest selection of reggae 45s and LPs in the South.

Euclid Records

3301 Chartres St.
Phone: 504-947-4348
Hours: 7 days a week: 11:00 a.m.–7:00 p.m.

The store recently moved next door to Pizza Delicious, the best pizza parlor in New Orleans. Euclid has an extensive collection of old and new vinyl, with about 80 percent of their inventory being from the '50s to recent releases. Longtime Vintage Vinyl employee James Weber left St. Louis for New Orleans. At Peaches Records on Decatur, he met Brian Bromberg, a New York transplant. Long story short, the result was Euclid Records.

"We just decided we could do it better," Weber says. They opened a store where they'd not only want to work but hang out. "You can go, stay as long as you want, no pressure. You can buy stuff, you can *not* buy stuff. You can talk about music, you can talk about whatever you want. It's that place to escape."

Guitar Center

1000 So. Clearview Pkwy #1040
Phone: 504-818-0336
Hours: Mon.–Sat.: 10:00 a.m.–9:00 p.m., Sun.:11:00 a.m.–7:00 p.m.

A chain of 260 stores with a wide selection befitting a chain.

International Vintage Guitars

3342 Magazine St.
Phone: (504) 442-0696
Hours: Mon.–Sat.: noon–6:00 p.m.

International Vintage Guitars offers vintage, used, and new guitars, amps, effects, and accessories. They are authorized dealers for Fender guitars and Fender parts and accessories, and guitars by Martin, Gretsch, Guild, National Resophonic, Jerry Jones, and Rickenbacker.

For more than 20 years, Steve Staples has been the proprietor. In the 1960s, Staples played with New Orleans teenage psych garage-rockers the Gaunga Dyns. The store was designed to be similar in spirit to the music stores of yesteryear, where both young and established musicians can hang out, trade licks, and talk shop. Visiting musical royalty like Bruno Mars, Billy Gibbons of ZZ Top, and Richie Havens frequent the store when they're in town.

Mushroom Records
1037 Broadway St.
Phone: 504-866-6065
Hours: 7 days a week: 10:00 a.m.–12:00 a.m.

The historic music/head shop has served the Tulane students and the New Orleans market since the 1970s. Walking by the psychedelic mural to take the stairs to the second story, the feeling is more '60s. My flashback, while being there, had me wonder what ever happened to my knee-high, lace-up, fringe boots, and purple bell bottom pants with the white pinstripes.

New Orleans Music Exchange
3342 Magazine St.
Phone: 504-891-7670
Hours: Mon.–Sat.: 10:30 a.m.–6:00 p.m., Sun.: 1:00–5:00 p.m.

The store sells all kinds of instruments, from new guitars to 80-year-old trombones. The feeling is like a musicians' pawn shop where a trumpet might be exchanged for the money to buy a line of cocaine. Not that that really happens.

Peaches Records
408 No. Peters St.
Phone: 504-282-3322
Hours: Mon.–Sat.: 10:00 a.m.–8:00 p.m., Sun.: 11:00 a.m.–7:00 p.m.

Back in the day, Peaches was a precursor of Tower Records, Media Play, Sam Goody, Turtles, and Virgin Megastores. They had stores in every major city. Each was a place you could buy anything that had to do with music, including concert tickets. The chain went bankrupt years ago. The New Orleans store is like a lone Japanese soldier burrowed into the hills who hasn't yet heard the war is over. Spend some time digging through half-empty bins and you might feel like you've arrived a few hours too late at a yard sale.

Ray Fransen's Drum Center
3412 Williams Blvd., Kenner, Louisiana
Phone: 504-466-8442
Hours: Mon.–Fri.: 10:00 a.m.–7:00 p.m.

Ray Fransen's Drum Center is the oldest and largest store in Louisiana dedicated exclusively to drums and drumming.

Skully'z Recordz
907 Bourbon St.
Phone: 504-592-4666
Hours: 7 days a week: 11:00 a.m.–8:00 p.m.

Skully'z is a small store with a large collection of CDs and vinyl. Their selections run the full range of music styles, and they're constantly changing those selections to focus on styles like indie, alternative, and hardcore rock.

APPENDIX C
THE BEST-OF LISTS

For *Eat Dat,* my book about New Orleans food culture, I closed the book with lists of BEST jazz brunch, BEST po'boys, BEST gumbo, and so forth. I used renowned food writers and experts like Poppy Tooker, Sara Roahen, Ian McNulty, and others to create those lists.

I wanted to do the same here using music critics, venerable record-store employees, radio DJs, and the like. But I found that it was hugely more difficult to pool their collective opinions. The following lists were created from the responses I did receive, supplemented by best-of lists posted by a few more learned websites. For this reason I have chosen not to provide the names of these responders here so that they won't be exposed, and perhaps then have to defend their choices.

As always, lists are created as much to create heated arguments as they are to lead you to treasured truths. I will forever go all crazy every time a Greatest Quarterback Ever list is posted and Otto Graham is missing. The man played 10 years of professional football, was in 9 championships, and won 7. Just because voters weren't alive to see him play doesn't mean he's irrelevant.

Note: the Top 20 to See & Hear Tonight list does not include some of our greats like Irma Thomas and Dr. John simply because their live performances are rare.

Top 20 Venues	Top 20 Historic Musicians	Top 20 to See & Hear Tonight
Tipitina's	Louis Armstrong	Rebirth Brass Band
Preservation Hall	Professor Longhair	Preservation Hall Band
The Spotted Cat	The Meters	Galactic
Snug Harbor	Sidney Bechet	Meschiya Lake
d.b.a.	Jelly Roll Morton	Kermit Ruffins
Blue Nile	Buddy Bolden	Anders Osborne
Maple Leaf Bar	James Booker	Big Freedia
One Eyed Jacks	Allen Toussaint	Little Freddie King
Howlin' Wolf	Mahalia Jackson	Wild Magnolias
BJ's	King Oliver	John Boutté
Bacchanal	Fats Domino	Helen Gillet
Three Muses	The Neville Brothers	Treme Brass Band
Little Gem Saloon	Irma Thomas	Soul Rebels

Fritzel's
Vaughan's
Chickie Wah Wah's
Hi-Ho Lounge
Irvin Mayfield's
Funky Pirate
House of Blues

Dr. John
Ernie K-Doe
Ellis Marsalis
Harry Connick Jr.
Pete Fountain
Kid Ory
Bunk Johnson

Rockin' Dopsie
Charmaine Neville
John Mooney
Amanda Shaw
Bonerama
Big Sam's Funky Nation
Tom McDermott

APPENDIX D
ESSENTIAL SONGS

I asked "expert" judges to whittle down a list of thousands upon thousands of great New Orleans songs to create this Essential Top 50 list. Remember, if you are enraged by any of these picks (or by songs left off the list), you need to raise hell with the judges (whom, as stated in Appendix C, I refuse to name). You might notice that "When the Saints Go Marching In" did not make this Top 50. Well, this Top 50 was compiled by people from New Orleans and suffice it to say we're all just a little weary of that song.

1.	Louis Armstrong	"Do You Know What It Means To Miss New Orleans"
2.	Professor Longhair	"Big Chief"
3.	Sugar Boy Crawford	"Jock-a-Mo"
4.	Fats Domino	"Walking to New Orleans"
5.	Louis Armstrong	"St. James Infirmary"
6.	The Meters	"Hey Pocky A-Way"
7.	Professor Longhair	"Go to the Mardi Gras"
8.	Louis Armstrong	"West End Blues"
9.	The Original Dixieland Jazz Band	"Tiger Rag"
10.	Dr. John	"Sweet Home New Orleans"
11.	Louis Armstrong	"Struttin' with Some Barbecue"
12.	Clarence Williams	"My Bucket's Got a Hole In It"
13.	Jelly Roll Morton	"Black Bottom Stomp"
14.	Rebirth Brass Band	"Do Watcha Wanna"
15.	Dr. John	"Right Place Wrong Time"
16.	Sidney Bechet	"Wild Cat Blues"
17.	The Meters	"Mardi Gras Mambo"
18.	Shirley & Lee	"Let the Good Times Roll"
19.	Professor Longhair	"Tipitina"
20.	The Wild Magnolias	"Handa Wanda"
21.	Allen Toussaint	"Southern Nights"
22.	Fats Domino	"Ain't That a Shame"
23.	Smiley Lewis	"I Hear You Knocking"
24.	Dixie Cups	"Chapel of Love"

25.	Huey "Piano" Smith	"Rockin' Pneumonia and the Boogie Woogie Flu"
26.	Danny Barker	"Tootie Ma Is a Big Fine Thing"
27.	Jelly Roll Morton	"New Orleans Blues"
28.	Wynton Marsalis	"The Majesty of the Blues (The Puheeman Strut)"
29.	King Oliver	"Dippermouth Blues"
30.	Louis Armstrong	"Heebee Jeebies"
31.	Dr. John	"Gris-Gris Gumbo Ya Ya"
32.	Rebirth Brass Band	"Do It Again"
33.	Lester Young	"Way Down Yonder in New Orleans"
34.	James Booker	"Gonzo"
35.	Jessie Hill	"Ooo Poo Pah Doo"
36.	The Iguanas	"Fortune Teller"
37.	Fats Domino	"The Fat Man"
38.	Clarence Frogman Henry	"Ain't Got No Home"
39.	Celestin's Original Tuxedo Jazz Orchestra	"Sing On"
40.	Kermit Ruffins	"Drop Me Off in New Orleans"
41.	Chris Kenner	"I Like It Like That"
42.	Red Allen	"It Should Be You"
43.	The Meters	"They All Ask'd For You"
44.	Al Johnson	"Carnival Time"
45.	John Boutté	"Foot of Canal Street"
46.	Nina Simone	"Little Liza Jane"
47.	Big Freedia	"Azz Everywhere"
48.	Louis Moreau Gottschalk	"Bamboula, Opus 2 (Danse des négres)"
49.	James Booker	"Papa Was a Rascal"
50.	Rebirth Brass Band	"Feel Like Funkin' It Up"

ACKNOWLEDGMENTS

I'd like to acknowledge the many, many fine musicians who will be out there performing tonight, tomorrow night, but who are not a part of *Hear Dat*. Sarah McCoy, Kidd Jordan, Johnny Sketch & the Dirty Notes, Dee-1, Dash Rip Rock, and Boyfriend, whatever her real name is, stand in for the hundreds more I wish I could have squeezed into these too-few pages. Hopefully, there'll be an updated edition so that I can add them.

I want to thank members of the band: Dan Crissman on editing, he often saved me from crossing the line between irreverent and snotty, Devorah Backman on publicity, Devon Zahn and Natalie Eilbert on production, and Ann Treistman as Countryman's publishing director. They were joined by the collaborative sounds of Bill Rusin and Michael Levatino and their chorus of sales professionals, with solos by Katie Cahill-Volpe, in special sales, and Beverly Benzeleski, handling the new accounts from the warehouse.

I approached photographer Marc Pagani almost at the last moment, and he was unavailable for a month, shooting overseas. But, as you have seen, he quickly accomplished excellent work and brought *Hear Dat* fully to life.

Once again, I am passionately grateful for the amazingly talented Stacie Herndon, who has done all three of the *Dat* covers and designed my website, www.alldat .guru. If you need some great work, check out her website, www.heelgrinder.com. Stacie was also chosen as my soul mate by one of those silly but addictive Facebook quizzes.

No offense to Facebook (nor Stacie) but I found my true soul mate back in 1996. Marnie Carmichael and I have now been married 15 years. Our wedding, held in New Orleans, was the best wedding I've ever been to. Kermit Ruffins was our wedding band. Rockin' Dopsie was our Friday night band.

I found my environs soul mate 13 years earlier when I visited New Orleans for the first time, May 1983. By the second day, I knew I was "home" and that I would someday live here. Now that I am here, I am never leaving, come hell or high water (the latter being quite possible).

I've written before, and I really do mean it, that I don't care if my book sells 300 copies or 30,000. Now, I prefer the second option and do appreciate royalty checks, but the experience of writing the book has already given me all that I need.

There have been so many great moments during the writing of *Hear Dat*. Marnie and I were overwhelmed watching the true artistry of Helen Gillet at the holy spot of Dew Drop Jazz Hall. When watching 70-year-old Cajun couples start executing perfect waltzes down the center aisle, we were literally in tears.

My lunch interview with Stanton Moore had the perfect closure when restaurant owner, Hugo Montero, stopped by to chat us up. Not recognizing each other at first, Hugo and Stanton came to realize they had lived right next door to one another some 20-plus years ago. Said Hugo, "Oh *you're* the guy that drove me *crazy* with all that drumming! I had kids that had to get to sleep."

Most cities are passionate about their sports teams, and New Orleans loves dem Saints. But no other city is as passionate about their music (and I include Nashville, Austin, Portland, Seattle, Chicago, and Motown). Just to be hooked into it a little more deeply during the writing of *Hear Dat* has been an utterly fulfilling experience.

I can't thank The Countryman Press enough for actually paying me to do it. I can never thank New Orleans enough for delivering the goods.

Music and rhythm find their way into the secret places of the soul.

—**Plato**

INDEX